# Death and Al

### Written By Christopher DeKleine

# Introduction

"Suffering itself has a way of opening our eyes to joys that we have never noticed before." - Jennifer Michael Hecht on Post Traumatic Bliss

In the year 2008 on the 10th of January, sixteen-year-old version of myself found his mom's ridged collapsed carcass on the laundry room floor with a grey nylon strap gripping her neck lassoed to the joist above. Within twenty-four hours, my father, a local police officer, confessed to murder and staging a suicide. Many misfortunes occurred in our little family before the murder: psychological disorders, suicide attempts, adultery, a tour of duty, separation, and divorce; many underlying events awaiting discovery to understand the childhood with which I am so graciously blessed. The journey has been long with elastic truths and answers begetting sleepless nights adding more questions. Too many to let it lie. Over many years, I interviewed family members and friends, read court documents, watched news videos, and meditated upon personal memories to formulate what is no longer a shaky idea of personal truth.

For a long time, I didn't know which parent to hate or love. First I blamed one then the other. There's been periods of both, but ended up landing on neither. When my father murdered my mother, it was really easy to point at him with blame because of the very obvious murder-victim mentality. Eventually it became clear the context of my childhood is complicated and confusing, concocting an emotional pancake, flip-flopping from one side to the other, raining blame like Lil' Wayne's strip club fund. But branding a new scapegoat is an act of condemnation and who am I, God? Santa Clause? Judges Dredd or Judy? No, no I am not. They both loved me in their own way despite the mass hysteria and confusion with which their love was partnered. Both of them are where they are now because of choices they made and the events that happened; some within, some without their control. The idea of this book was conceived as a way to organize my understanding of these choices and consequences and maybe even figure out what the hell happened in my life and for the love of God, why it happened. Maybe through my personal experiential truths, universals will arise from this chaos.

    Like two protons colliding, sending quarks and gluons careening every which way, so does a tragic event send everyones personal lives and fractured psyches. Some people got angry, some sad, some confused, sometimes all of these flying around bashing each other like a Quidditch match of feels. The death of my mom happened at the comical peak of the whole "Your Mom" meme and despite frequent reminders of what happened, I refused to perpetuate the victim mentality. Instead of stewing in perceived misfortune, I swim, I soak, I bask, I laugh in it. No person, action, or event can bring me down unless I let it, which is why much of this will be politically incorrect and mildly offensive, especially to those who were close to the situation. This is for entertainment purposes both for myself in the writing process and the reader in the reading process, as well as a tool to negate the victim mentality through humor, regardless of how crude it may sound.

    My dad wrote in one of his letters, which are

dispersed throughout this book:

*Your passion for letters I have not forgotten but I don't think anyone will be putting together a book about letters from prison.*

Well here I am dad, writing a book using your letters from prison. There were lots of them and were what inspired me to forgive both parents and eventually reconnect with the remaining. My aunt and uncle graciously saved and safely stowed these letters until I was emotionally savvy and let me know they were there when I needed them. For that, I am grateful. I have read all of them, but chose the ones that inspired and taught most. In this book are both letters from him to various people in his life and journals from my mom, which were kept in evidence and obtained through the Freedom of Information Act (free my ass, I had to pay for that). The names have been changed and irrelevant details eschewed, but the words are his and no idea has been altered.

When I told my dad about this book and after he shed a few tears he said to me, "You are the one that has to be doing this. If anyone else did, no one would understand." He's not saying I have such a gift of gab that I am born to be a writer. He is saying I have the right to say these things because I was in the thick of the shit, and people will listen to a """"victim"""". I loved my mom with all my heart- she was my home- and it sucks on the regular when I don't get to tell her about all my adventures and it took years of psychological adjustment. For instance -after she died- when I would do something cool, I would think, "Man, I can't wait to tell my Mo...damn." She was a great person, even better listener and it sucks that he killed her. In order to forget hatred and forgive, one must first understand. Forgiveness is not excuse of a transgression but choosing not to live with hatred. Otherwise it bleeds into all aspects of life and will affect every single one of your decisions. Trust. Me. None more please thank-you.

One recurring idea in my letters and expressed in the media (one of the few things they got right) is how my father's motivation was out of love for my sister and I. Leading my search to start out with one question: "How can he murder and justify it with love?" This twisted tuning fork of irony rang true. How can a human think this way? Are there others that have done the same? Was my perspective of the situation wrong and was he somehow right? Murder is no easy act and doesn't come to fruition easily, so how could he jump to such an vile extreme?

Turns out my mother had some pretty serious issues with mental illness. Some of which psychiatrists and psychologists barely understand and neither did the rest of the family, especially my dad. Many of the unsavory actions she took were not direct choices but derived from clinically diagnosed disorders, although that is still not an excuse. Since these mental problems are unknown and under researched, no one knew how to identify or act which led to dire consequences. No one is to blame; we are all victims and when everyone is a victim, no one is a victim.

Sure he murdered my mother but it is not a black and white situation. My mother was not everything she said she was and my father was no different. In his letters, he makes it clear he believes he did the right thing and knew what would happen to my sister and I when he strangled my mother. It was a conscious decision which he believed would make my life better. After everything happened, my sister and I moved in with our aunt and uncle, who showed us nothing but love. When he says killing my mother would give me a better life, I can't say he is wrong but in order to understand, you have to know what it was like before it all happened.

*January 1993* (a year and a half after I was born)
*Dear Christopher,*

*Lately I've been thinking about what I should be doing to make sure good values are taught to you by myself. What can I do to teach you those values? How can I best demonstrate them to you by my actions? What priority should each value have relative to the others.*

*I think the most important thing for me to realize is that I will not be teaching you all the values you learn. There will be countless other influences in your life that effect your choices. The best I can hope for is to do myself what I can and after that make sure the environment you mature in is of a good Christian value oriented setting. Like a Company Commander, who is responsible for everything in the company but can't do it all. He has to make sure those he entrusts with his soldiers have the same goals and intent he has.*

*As for my actions demonstrating my values, I pray that you are blessed with good judgement. Son, I'm not perfect, you will have to look to me with an eye that can disregard the bad and pick out the good. I have pledged that I will do my best at your baptism and am reminded of that every time I witness another baptism. God has loaned you to me so I try to think of that every time I have to make a choice.*

*What I put as my highest priority is probably how I will effect you without you even knowing. I hope you always feel that next to God in my heart, you, as a part of my family, are the most important thing to me. When you read this I hope you will think I haven't been too mixed up. I'm sure you can think of times I was wrong but over all I hope not.*

*- Dad*

# 6

After the first draft of this manuscript was finished I sent it to my dad in prison. He took a good six months to read and respond. When I got his response, my idea of what I thought this book would be was shattered yet again. So I decided to include a lot of his revisions without necessarily changing what I wrote and consider it a dialogue because that has been what this is a all about: a dialogue between a father and a son trying to figure out where it went all wrong so we can live together in harmony. You know, like ebony and ivory. A cowriter was not expected on this project but that is now what I consider him, despite his humility on the matter. Unless of course he's not legally aloud to produce things like this from the inside, in which case this is all me in character and this novel is fiction.

*By sending me your manuscript and asking me for comments and input, you are learning that you have found the the tipping point of my angle of repose that caused this avalanche of massive amounts of feedback. It's probably because you are doing more than just enabling me to live vicariously through your writing, but avatar for me and do it better than I ever could have done and accomplish so much more of what I wish I could do, but am not able to.*

*This may seem like an overwhelming amount of a response to what you sent me and asked of me, but believe me, I write slowly and labor over what I write even though it may not seem so. (**ARGH! My only fine tipped pen finally ran out. I have more coming but who knows when I'll get them.**) Furthermore, I spend more time pondering about what to write then actually writing. I feel that you and I communicating with each other about what you've written will tighten and strengthen the fibers of our lives together rather than leaving them like a crewel led or* *frayed worsted yarn, tattered by time and separation. A big reason I want to put my best effort into the feedback I give you is that I deeply appreciate you bearing your soul, expressing brutal honesty, and pouring your guts out for others to see in an effort to help them understand that there are not always answers to everything (koans), especially when it comes to dealign with loved ones with mental illness. It sure has helped me appreciate the tensile strength of your character. Now I am eviscerating myself for you and the world to see too. But mostly to you, and for you.*

*We were both caught up in the warp and woof of a fabric that neither of us could alter the way we would have liked to have been able to. Now we find ourselves in a mutuality that has tied us in a single garment even though it seems to have been rendered apart by distance. Your manuscript, like the signal fire Pippin lights on top of Minis Tirith in <u>Lord of the Rings,</u> that carried the message over the cordillera to Rohan, your efforts have done so much to mend what I rent apart.*

*Thank you for this expression of your love.*

# Chapter 1: Childhood Insanity

*Memories of Toph,*
 *It's hard to say sometime exactly what motivates us to pick up a particular habit or action when we are very young, but most of us have something we can remember doing that we did for a while. When I was three or four someone must have praised me for how well I could make graham cracker crumbs. It may have been [Aunt] or a friend of hers that showed me how to rub two graham crackers together and make crumbs. After I tried it, someone (probably whoever taught me) praised me and said what a good job I did making the crumbs. Stupid, I know, but I loved doing that with graham crackers for a long time after that. For no reason at all I would lay the two crackers flat on the table as I was shown and rub the edges together grinding them into crumbs. Wow! Why do we do what we do at that young age.*
 *I assume someone may have praised you for closing a food container on the dinner table because for a while, that was your thing. You made sure that all of the covers of the food containers had their covers on if it was not being used. You must have been only two or three because you were still sitting in the high chair when we ate at the dinner table. You've never been one to say much at the table but at that age you hardly ever talked, but it was always obvious that your mind was working. I remember once when we were having hamburgers or hotdogs and we had all the condiments on the table. After everyone was done preparing their hotdogs and started eating, suddenly you were a boy with a mission. You started to climb out of you high chair and on to the table. I couldn't figure out what you were up to until you closed the ketchup container, then*

*the mustard, and then whatever else was not covered. I couldn't help but take notice of what you were doing and notice that you did that for several meals after that. I just tried to get in the habit of covering everything when we were done with it so you wouldn't be crawling across the table because of your focusing on a ketchup bottle that was open. For you it was easier to take care of it yourself then to ask someone to close it.*

*It's just before Christmas so I've been doing thinking about some of the Christmas memories I have of you. It must have been the Christmas of 2001 or 2002 when you got your second Gameboy. The first one you got was the Christmas or birthday of 1999. I can remember that you got it that year because they were a really popular gift but they were very hard to come by. They were hard to find because the screens for them were made at a factory in Turkey and Turkey had had a very bad earthquake that year that destroyed the factory. Since the screens couldn't be made for a while there was a shortage of Gameboys in the stores. I'm glad you didn't know how lucky you were to get a Gameboy that year because then all you had was the pure enjoyment and excitement of getting a gameboy. Actually I'm not sure if you got your first one for Christmas or your Birthday but like I started this paragraph out with, you got your second one for Christmas which I know for sure.*

*After you had your first Gameboy stolen at church I could not wait for you to get another one because you loved having your first one so much and played it all the time. I don't know who was looking forward to you opening that Christmas present more, me or you. Everything seemed to revolve around Gameboys for a while. Like when we were in Colorado with the Calvin group. There you sat in the back of the van with [your friends] playing Gameboy as we drove through the mountains. [My friend] and I just shook our heads and amazement at what you boys found interesting. Oh well, it was still a lot of fun watching you kids together. Like when a bunch of you had a "fort" outside our cabin and you couldn't wait to get back from rafting or wherever so you could play there some more. I regretfully remember when I made Bre so mad at me because of her Gameboy. We were going somewhere for an appointment and as usual we were running a little late. When we got there, Bre was playing her Gameboy and still had to put her shoes on. When we got there and she wouldn't stop playing her Gameboy I pulled the game cartridge out. Boy was she ever mad at me! I guess I could have handled that much better.*

*I bet you don't remember getting your Fischer Price lawn mower. I think you were only three or four at the time. At first I couldn't wait for the next summer so you could take it outside but then you had some fun with it inside the house anyway. That was pre-Bionicles for you and just about the time when Bre was into Barbies.*

*Let me see how many of the things you got into for a while that I can list. I think the first was Legos. After that came Beanie Babies, Bionicles, Pogs, and Pokemon cards. Those are all the fads I can think of right now. Thinking back on how driven you were to get those things even at that age, I hope you never lose that. Your ability to make goals and focus on them has always been a blessing.*

*Dad's Letter*
*Thursday June 19, 2008*
*Dear Topher,*
 *I think of you often and pray for you often as well. You have given me and all those that love you so much to be proud of you for. You are so gifted and smart and yet so*

*easy going and likable. You always have been that way. I'll never forget about the time you told me about finding [Hoss] crying behind the soccer wall at Pine Ridge Christian School in fourth or fifth grade because nobody would play with him. When you told me that you talked to him and asked him to come and play with you and some of your friends, I was amazed. Being smart is one thing but to see how you have used your head to help others is something I think God has really blessed you with the ability to do. After you took big [Hoss] under your wing, you had a very devoted friend for a while. You may not be friends anymore but I'm sure he will never forget what you did for him that day. He will remember that you like you will remember "what's his name" through your Rugrats hat out the bus window. Remember how we went looking for it right away and found it laying in the ditch or on the side of the road? You loved that hat and I was so happy for you when we found it.*

*I saw this article about Dr. Carson in the paper a few days ago. When I saw his picture I recognized him right away as the doctor feature in one of your school papers years ago. I think I remember how that article in your school paper made quite an impression on you, if I remember right. I forgot all about him until I saw his picture and read the article. And if I had to guess, this guy is the one that started you thinking about being a neurosurgery doctor. That is a great goal. Go for it!*

*Uncle Keith said you are going down to Chicago on a mission trip again. It's great that you have that group of friends that you can hang out with and do stuff like that. Doing service projects like that and selfless acts like with [Hoss] are things that will give you a good reputation and get you a long way in life. You are already known for being Christ-like and I know that is because you let God use you any way He wants.*

*Right now I have to remember, as hard as that is, to think ahead about how God may use me. There are some things I have to get straightened around first but I hope to get there some day soon. I have a good example in you for that even though you may not think it. I clearly can picture you at nine years old in 2001, down in Tijuana, playing with Bomarro. I may have done a lot of physical work on the mission there but you may have left a bigger impression than a lot of us. You may have been bored but you never complained. That was such a cool trip except for having to say goodbye to the other kids and go to Disneyland.*

*I hope you can remember well all of the good times we had and forgive me for the bad things Iv'e done. That goes for things in the past and more recently. I have to learn to forgive myself for some things yet, but I keep trying. It makes me sad to think about how many hours you spent in that swing as a baby but you were always so content to swing for hours watching Bre or whatever else was going on. That's why it amazes me how social you are. Not needing to be the center of attention but none the less, you like to be in the activity it seems.*

*I love you bud. Take care and remember how many other people love you too.*

*Love Dad*

Although my parents consistently insisted upon it, a compassionate little angel I was not. In fifth grade, I was a literal balls-kicking bully. Recall that point in my dad's letter about befriending the "big kid" in school. Well, he only knew half of that story. There was only one kid I picked on relentlessly. He was a portly boy we'll call Hoss, who was much bigger than me. He didn't have any friends so he latched himself to the periphery of my group while we used his pain for our amusement and turned him into a class clown. It ended up needing to get physical before I realized what was going on and how awful of a person into which I was morphing.

There was a wall at our elementary school where kids would frolic and kick soccer balls against. One of the games we played was a gauntlet challenge where one person would run across the wall, while others would carefully aim and kick the ball. It was Hoss's turn more often than not but he acted like he enjoyed it so we became incredibly encouraging asshats all of a sudden.

Until one day I took things a little too far. We were just kickin' it per the usual when Hoss started getting too close to my real friends and I told him to scram. When he didn't listen, I kicked him right in the gonads as hard as I could. Apparently that sucked for him, so he ran around the corner in tears with my friends behind me in laughs. Something was obviously wrong when the bell rang and he didn't come back. I genuinely thought he liked that sort of attention. I traced his path and saw him hunched against the school wall crying. In relation to time, the pain to nut kick ratio had long subsided so I knew he wasn't crying from anything physical.

With genuine curiosity, I sat beside him and asked him what was wrong. Through wet cheeked stutters, he ended up revealing all he was trying to do was make friends because he had none. *I don't know what asshole means yet, but I'm pretty sure I'm that.* I wholeheartedly apologized and told him I would convene with my friends and make them understand. That's exactly what we did. After recess, in the classroom, my pals gathered and I told them what had happened and what he said. They understood and agreed to invite him to play with us next time in a less painful manor. And so began a beautiful relationship.

Turns out Hoss was a pretty fun guy. We invited him over to our respective houses and vis versa. Turns out he had an X-box, which we were all geeked about and led to many sleepless nights playing Soul Caliber. What could be better than disproportionate hot chicks and kung fu? There was one fighting girl character we called "Jiggly" because obvious parts of her anatomy jiggled when she punched or kicked or if there was a slight breeze or the slightest modicum of movement. Naturally she was chosen every round.

As we went into middle school, things changed and we went our different ways. I was a soccer player; he was a football player. Some friendships just can't work out. We'd talk in class and in the halls but he made other friends through his extracurriculars and I was happy for him. I take credit in helping him find his way, building his confidence or some shit, but only a little. His current whereabouts are unknown but he will always be considered a positive influence in my life for helping me discover empathy and compassion. When I told my dad this story, I would leave out the first part, the part where I was a horse's ass. I did tell him the truth eventually and he just replied with a "Huh." Silence. Then burst into laughter.

*Mom's Journal*
*No Date*
   *When I was a little girl...*

   *I marvel at the innocence of youth.*
   *Playing house, dodging in and out of the sprinkler, hiding and seeking, throwing the "lid" to Rusty, running, biking, all the things you could want for a carefree childhood. Laughing, screaming, yelling at will and with*

*great liberty.*

*Knocking on the door of one or more of the neighbor kids, asking if they could play. There were so many doors with so many children to revel in any of the joys of youth.*

*Somehow, almost like a whisper, we all sorta grow up. Playing house fades as dolls are tucked away. Sprinklers are only good for watering the lawn; a friends swimming pool is just a bike ride away. Old games get boring, likely replaced by a good TV Show. Rusty eventually dies and his owners move away. Running and biking become exercise and a means to go somewhere else.*

*The kids behind the doors grow up too, like me, like you.*

*The innocence and freedom of youth get tucked away somewhere, becoming memories of another time far far away to when I was a little girl.*


*Mom's Journal*
*July 31, 2007*
    *What I remember is that I must have been a royal pain in the ass to a lot of people, always looking for an ear or a shoulder of someone who actually gave a shit. Yet they were there, if only for a short time, before most of them burned out. I remember feeling lost, confused, hopeless, staring for something that spoke deep down inside me. I just couldn't figure it out. I remember sitting at a kitchen table while our toddlers played cheerfully in the other room. I remember [Friend] being a very wise woman as I bore my struggles to her. There were others along the way, but the answers were not in them any more than they were in me. I remember my confusion which constantly put me in a state of funk to the point of hopeless unworthy existence that just wouldn't pass away from me no matter what meds*

*I took or which doctor I saw or how hard I prayed, begged God to make it stop. It plagued me year after year with no end in site. I remember knowing my "Old self" of youth-vibrant, funny, smart, creative, involved in anything and everything. I remember her, but no matter how hard I tried I could not resurrect her. A tiny mustard seed in me held fast that said that there was hope, a plan, a purpose. A mustard seed is as big as a grain of pepper.*

*I don't remember what happened when I gave up completely. Just could not take one more step. I just wanted to go home, to my real home where I had to believe I would be forgiven of whatever sin had caused my misery and that this welcome would be with the open arms of Jesus himself. This world is not my home. I know that I took a small handful of some "leftovers" in my cupboard swallowing them all at once with a glass of wine. I was a corpse. I fell asleep, but I don't remember being rushed by ambulance to the hospital or having my stomach pumped or having my clothes exchanged for a gown, or having a catheter put in. I don't remember someone's kind words of love and assurance. I don't remember being attended by anyone. I just don't remember. I don't remember the point at which I realized "damnit" I had survived. I don't remember when my thoughts became remotely clear. I don't remember being transferred to the psych ward or who may have been with me. I certainly don't remember feeling love from anywhere.*

*What I wish I could forget is how when it was time for me to rejoin my family, I was scared! No more controlled environment, group therapy, regular meals, hurting people, doctor consults, efforts to make sense of anything. I wish I could forget the silence of walking to the car. I wish I could forget sitting in the passenger seat, terrified, looking out the window at God knows what. I wish I could forget that* moment where the car paused before leaving the parking lot. I wish I could forget his harsh words, "I am so angry. If you ever try something like this again, you're not coming home." I wish I could forget that those words came from someone who was supposed to love me for better or for worse. I wish I could forget how badly I wanted to open my car door at any point on the drive home- to just fall out while we were in motion or just jump out and run. I wish I could forget that no one brought my children to see me. I wish I could forget how all alone I felt. I wish I could forget. I just wish I could forget.

But if I did, how could I ever discover myself as I am now? I am fulfilling my purpose little by little. I will never again be at that point of remembering or not wanting to remember. I am me.

*Mom's Journal*
*April 18, 2007*
*Day Tripper, take the easy way out.*

It took me so long to find out, but I found out that there is no easy way out, whether I'm a day tripper or not. What the heck is a day tripper anyways? I suppose if you were a Beatle, you would be tripping quite a bit, perhaps even week tripping on some pink elephant floating in the sky. "Hey Lucy, nice diamonds! That's a very good choice." She waves like a queen on a float wearing a dopey sort of smile. Definitely trippin' for some amount of time.

Let's peek in on Eleanor Rigby, the poor dear. No easy way out for her. Imagine that jar by her door; I wonder what the mask actually looked like. Something tells me that she wasn't doing a lot of tripping, except perhaps if she somehow forgot about that jar as she was heading out, smashing her real face onto the floor. Poor Eleanor. No *friends, no family that even showed up at any significant even in her life, spare the priest, but I suppose he was either paid pretty well or he was on a trip of his own.*

*There's just no easy way out. No matter what, the tripping' eventually lulls or halts and not even the yellow submarine can help you escape that. It's too crowded with all the people living in there anyways.*

*And really, I think we'll just all learn at one point there's no easy way out. I just found that out.*

Man. That's depressing. I've read over that so many times and cannot help but come to the conclusion the only reason I, or anyone else for that matter, spent time around her was because of pity. It is impossible for any of us to know whether or not it was an unconscious or subconscious decision; whether it was disorder or manipulation. All I can do is call it like I see it and all I see is sadness. While empathy leads to understanding, but pity is purely driven by selfishness. "Oh look at that sad girl, she must need a friend." No that is just the soft bigotry of low expectation, they can help themselves. What will end up happening is you go out of your way in a vain attempt to cheer them up. Because happiness comes only from within, it never works and now you've created an extra unsatisfied soul that is yourself.

Insane may be a strong word but considering what my parents did to each other, it is both correct and unpleasant. Lori- Mom- was in and out of psychiatric clinics and on and off medications, institutionalized by clinics and her own mind- having been diagnosed with multiple psychological disorders including Bipolar and Borderline Personality Disorder. My Father killed someone, which is an extreme act to say the least and isn't something a completely sane person does. Although his insanity was circumstantial, hers was clinically persistent.

Growing up with increasingly mutually exclusive parents clinging to the outskirts of sanity land wasn't all bad news bears. They taught me many memorable lessons that guide me today and even though I don't always like to admit it, I am very similar to both of them. While their insanity was incredibly blatant in the end, there was not much evidence of it growing up. Thanks to their care on what to exhibit, I was able to be a child when I was a child... mostly. Sure I found my mom crying a lot and visited her in hospital after secret suicide attempts, but these things occurred behind closed doors while on the other side was Tiny Topher pleasuring himself on a heaping pile of Pokemon Cards. Perhaps the ignorance was my own, perhaps it was their concerned planning that kept me in the dark, perhaps it was a cocktail of the two and more. Either way, I was able to have a fantastic childhood and looking back, I wouldn't change a thing. Gratitude is within every moment.

Since the day I was born, I was a Momma's Boy- clinging to her leg like a Koala. On top of that ice cream was a maraschino cherry of loathing I held for my father. So much so, I would actively avoid him. Every two weeks, like a Type A clock, he would write his work schedule on the family calendar and, after the room cleared, I would sneak in a la Tom Cruise Mission Impossible to investigate when he would be at work and I could have fun. Obviously I knew this wasn't okay, otherwise I wouldn't have been so sneaky. Second shift was my favorite because then he wouldn't be there when I got home from school, allowing me to play my Gameboy without guilt until my eyes bled. I'm not sure why this happened but I'll bet Siggy Freud has something to say about it.

There's no doubt about it, my mom was my best

friend; I could tell her anything. Well, except for the one time the name of a porno came up on "Recently Played" in Windows Media Player while she was trying to show me a funny video. There was only silence. Silence and a slow movement towards the X on the top right of the screen. I broke the silence with a "Huh, I wonder how that got there, that's weird." *Ya, sure, she totally believed you, I guarantee it.* Turns out she did believe me and blamed it on my dad.

*WAIT JUST A SECOND!!! A porno came up on the computer as "Recently Played" when mom was on the computer with you? This is one instance where the sins of the son rain down upon the father instead of the other way around. You know she blamed me for that, right? If not for having been the one to view the video but for having been the one to introduce you to it. You... turd bird! I'll consider that payback from you for something else. There was a time I found some lesbian porn on the computer once. It wasn't me. Was that you? I blamed that on mom, but then again, I had reason to blame her given her and Barb. That is all so ironic! I'm laughing so hard inside at the irony that my eyes are weeping.*

Uhhhhhhhh...... Whoops. Don't watch porn kids. For the record though, my dad did not introduce me to porn. I was a budding young man, the very fires of Hell couldn't keep me from looking at some titties.

The point still remains. I told mom everything. Even my friends would come over specifically to talk to her because she was a judgement-free listener who gave great advice. That and my house was known as the house at which you could curse your fucking brains out. For a freshmen in Holland Christian High School, this was a big deal.

That girl was my go-to gal. If my dad was the one to tuck me in, I would sigh and moan and request otherwise, which is why an alternating tuck-in schedule had to be implemented. I would even force her to sit and guard my open bedroom door while I worried about being able to fall asleep, only to frequently peek open an eye to make sure she was at her post. My fear of being able to fall asleep would often keep me up and the only thing that would allow slumber was the comfort of my parents' water bed. It would usually take me a while to conquer my fear and gather the courage to enter their room. I would stand outside the door and count to ten in my head, telling myself once I reached ten, I would enter. Of course this would happen three or four times before I would euphemise "Screw it" and enter. My dad had no blind eye to this momma's boy dilemma so he would make obvious attempts to counter it. Which only made me back away more because I didn't know his attempts were accompanied with good intention and a dollop of desperation.

Seriously, I have no idea where this distaste for my own father came from. During the trial, the words "victim" and "domestic abuse" were tossed around like pizza dough. Fake News existed long before the 2016 presidential elections. It was clear they used these key words and Dad's trashed name to create a narrative that attracted viewership. Sad. My dad was the least violent man I knew. He played soccer for Christ's sake. He was a mild mannered Dutchman at worst.

Apparently he was one of the best cops in town. His old boss, the police chief, told me Ken would often get in trouble for not writing enough tickets. His ex-boss also told the local news, "The guy loved everybody. You saw him serving kids food, helping fix bikes; he cared." He made sure to know the people on his block and had genuine care for them. The chief goes on, "But obviously he suppressed something so deep inside of him that bothered him so much to commit such an act." Fay Key, a frequently visited elderly woman from his beat and his self-proclaimed friend told me in an interview, "It was just a comfort knowing he's out there" and "he's not just a regular cop."

After the murder, many people considered him a narcissistic psychopath. Being a policeman? That was clearly for attention. Going to Iraq? Definitely a selfish prick. Trying to get custody of his own children? So obvious he doesn't know it's the current year. Trying to oust inappropriate sexual relations with a therapist? Morally abhorrent. Having coffee with an old women? The gaul of this man. Nobody even knew about the Fay Key visits, so what could he possibly be gaining from secretly visiting an old lady? Even now, in prison, he is working with the Calvin College prison ministry program and his name has been in the papers and news several times because of the greatness coming from it. Upon the latest visit, I mentioned this and he had no idea he was being noticed. The man's newsworthy, plain and simple.

My father tried so hard, even desperately. He would not only ask me to play with him, but would always make sure it was something I wanted to do first. At the time I thought he was trying to force something on me, but since then realized that he never pressured me to do anything, but encouraged me to find things I enjoyed that weren't sitting on the couch watching TV or playing Pokemon on my beloved Gameboy. We tried Aikido, a defensive form of martial arts together. It was held at the church across the street by some dude with a mustache. I had an interest in it for a while and so did he. As I witnessed him getting better than me, I started to get sick of it and back away. He once invited me to Aikido night and I blamed the inability to attend on my heaping loads of homework. I was in sixth grade and it was for art class. My homework was literally draw a picture of whatever I want and, for those wondering, it happened to be a Homer Simpson portrait. This was a cheap excuse; he knew it and I knew it. So he did the right thing and confronted me in a calm manor with slight exasperation saying, "If you don't want to go, that's all you have to say." I was afraid to be honest because I knew the real reason I didn't want to go was because he was there.

Many times I actually wished and granted physical harm on the poor bastard. We used to have a weekly, pick-up, street hockey game in the church parking lot across the road from our house. At first it was the pastor's job to organize it, but as he grew older and busier, I took over the whole ordeal. He blamed it on tennis elbow. Tennis elbow. TENNIS elbow. He was supposed to be a real hockey player- from Canada and everything. TENNIS ELBOW. Just kidding buddy, you were an inspiration and I just wanted you on the rink to give me a real challenge. I still let my ego run rampant with pride in my ability to gather a neighborhood of children and adults to come play hockey with me, which is all I ever wanted. I was the head honcho; people came to me to see if hockey was on. If I didn't play, no one played. Toot toot- that's my own horn. It's not because I had the hockey nets in my garage, I swear.

On one particular summer hockey eve, my father had gotten angry at me. I had taken one of his screw drivers and failed to return it to the proper place on the shelf. So when he needed it, it wasn't there and was left scouring the ceaseless abyss that was our garage. He expressed mild frustration but it was all I could focus on. He said what was on his mind, inflicted no punishment, and put on his hockey gear.

However, I was not on that page and chose to let the matter fester and ferment my mind-grapes. He made me feel shame and must be held accountable, preferably in a physical way and I knew how to play hockey better more than I knew how to make a shiv. Not to mention the reason he got so frustrated was because leaving belongings of other people's out of place happened to be a honed habit of mine. I did what any man of salt would do: I swallowed my anger and puked it out on the hockey rink. We tossed the sticks into the sorting pile and I carefully sorted ours into opposite teams. Since he had started rollerblading late in the hockey game of life, he was a very uncoordinated person and just plain awful on wheels. I bladed circles around the guy while viciously hacking at his shins whenever he was unfortunate enough to get the ball.

After all the hacking, skating, and falling, my dad got tired and volunteered to be goalie. *My plan is working perfectly. I am a golden god, destroyer of worlds, shatterer of shins.* I didn't care about scoring although I aimed carefully and precisely: for the shins, the knees, the balls. If I scored, I failed. I was pretty damn good too so it wasn't often I missed. His legs were so covered in red spots, the church almost sent him to a leper colony on the outskirts of Beersheba. One shot went right in between his legs and was caught in between his monstrous calf muscles. He humorously hollered in pain and while my team was let down, I saw the red marks and let out a shifty-eyed grin.

*Dad's Letter*
*November 17, 2008*
*My thankful memories of Christopher,*
*During the summer of 1992 our family stayed over night at Grandma and Grandpa's. We slept in the green tent just north of the garage. During the night you started to fuss a little bit because you were only about nine months old at most. Plus, a big thunderstorm came through that night with all kinds of thunder and lightning. The only way*

*you would sleep was on my bare chest and with you in only your diaper. You slept the whole night, that I can remember, curled up in a ball on my chest. We stayed out there through the storm and everything. As you slept the wind was blowing so hard that I had to push the side of the tent off of you. The rain was hitting so hard that it came through both layers of the tent as a mist. As bad as it was out, I could not have been happier with you, son, sleeping on my chest through all that. I felt that God had blessed me so much then and I still feel that he has blessed me now with a son like you. Plus, not only did he bless me, He also blessed so many other people with you too.*

*I remember so well taking you home after picking up your glasses. I had never had glasses yet so I could not relate to not being able to see well but it was amazing to hear you tell me what you could see then that you could not have seen before. It was so cool to hear you read signs and billboards that you couldn't read before. I think that was the summer of 2004, right after your sixth grade year.*

*I never gave it a second thought, the day you came home from the Tot Lot wearing that PRINCE baseball caps. You had not been a hat wearer before but you wore that hat like white on rice. After that you got your RugRats hat and you wore that hat all the time until the time it went out the bus window when that little bugger threw it out. I never told you but I had dealt with that kids family while I was working so I knew trying to deal with him or his parents was a dead end. That is why I so desperately wanted to find that hat along the side of the road. I was so happy for your sake when we found it. I knew how much that hat meant to you. Not only that, but I can imagine what it felt like to have a bully grab your favorite hat off your head and throw it out the window. That may have been the worse part. I remember very well when someone on my school bus spit in the back of my hair. And my mom or dad was the bus driver! But in your situation, if I remember right, that jerk that took your hat never did anything to you like that again. You were upset when you came home off the bus but it all turned out well.*

*You've always had such a great group of friends that were fun to have come over. [The twins] could be a bit much at times but it would always be worth it. The best time I remember when you got a bunch of friends together was when you had a day off from school on a snow day. You called a bunch of kids to go sledding and we had burgers and hot chocolate at Van Raalte Farm hills. That was so fun for me, watching you kids have so much fun. It was a perfect snowy day to be out there and God allowed us to make the best of it. Not many kids at the age you were then would have been able to pull that off and get so many friends to come out like that but you are well liked and smart.*

*Of course I remember when you became friends with that big kid in your class. You said you found him alone and upset behind the soccer wall at Pine Ridge. You must have been in fourth or fifth grade I think. When you asked him what was the matter, he told you that nobody wanted to play with him. You took him in, included him, and he looked up to you as a friend for a long time after that. I'm not sure what kind of a kid he is now but I'd bet you anything that he remembers that day and what you did very well.*

*Do you remember that matching game you had when you were in preschool? You could always do so well with that! It had the animals on one side of the cardboard squares. You could make those matches so well that it amazed me then and it still does. That was when I started to realize how very much God had blessed you with intelligence. But it's not only being smart that you amazed me with but your drive to work for things and to do the right thing.*


Dad's Letter
Excerpt from March 30, 2008
Dear Bre and Toph,
    *I like to think about the diamond memories I have of different things we did. Driving down to Tijuana in 2001. Toph, you were so sad to say good-bye to the youth group, even though we were going to Disney the next day. You had stayed out almost all night the night before with the boys to walk to the pier in San Diego. Bomarro- playing with him at the mission. Bre, you worked so hard with all the high school kids.*
    *I laugh about the time you had a bunch of the Chorale Kids girls over night after the last Tulip Time performance. I just laughed and told so many people how cool that was.*
    *How about the time we went up to [a friend's] trailer in Pentwater? Just as we load up to come home, Toph blows off the Stink Bomb in the van that you got in the store or somewhere. Man did that reek!!*
    *How about this? "We are not lost in this canyon!" We're about to drop over from thirst but "we are not lost." Hahaha What a jerk! I'm glad you guys didn't panic.*
    *Bre, remember watching that lightning storm over Denver when we camped out at the waterfalls at Snow Mountain Ranch? That is one of the coolest things I have ever seen. That was in 1997!*
    *Sleeping in the snow caves, sledding party cook outs at Van Raalte Farms Hill. Toph, remember when you fell in the river during that winter hike at Van Raalte Farms? You were incredibly tough and made it all the way back to the*

*van on your own.*
*I could go on and on with all the memories of the blessing we have had. God blessed the four of us in so many ways. I try not to forget that or even let it fade but sometimes life gets so crazy and it's easy to forget. I pray that the both of you can go on making memories of your own that will be good and meaningful for a long time.*
*I love you guys!*
*Love Dad*


When I was young, I loved hats. Specifically a blue Rugrats hat. I wore it everyday all day; it was my savior, my life partner, my everything. One day while riding the bus, one of my miscreant friends grabbed my hat and started tossing it around as if it wasn't made out of love platinum. Frantically I leapt every which way in hopes of returning it to my head- its home. Unfortunately the bus window behind one of them was open and with one unlucky toss it went careening outside along with my well-wishes and happiness. Oh, the hat-manity. Pain and sadness began to boil within. An emotional grenade had exploded with ringing ears and slow motion, the whole deal. The rest of the bus ride is a bar top bowl of sadness and hatred, love lost and dwindled hope. After trudging home, I unveiled the horror to my dad and he immediately grabbed the car keys, while I tried to retain as much dignity and situational awareness as possible. Since I was young and ignorant, I had no idea what streets were on the route or where the hat remained. One of the terrorists involved in this atrocity got off at the same stop as me but but he felt bad so he became our spirit guide to ground zero. Bless him. We found the hat strewn on the side of the road like an abandoned Chinese baby girl. The brim had been snapped in half and was smudged with dirt. None of this mattered though; I had my hat back. The hat was donned as I slowly raised my arms to the shape of a cross while bright lights behind silhouetted the moment of reconnection.

    Both my parents made a fantastic attempt at showing my sister and I the vast cultures of Planet Earth. Even when we were really young, they took us on mission trips to the depraved lands of The Dominican Republic, Tijuana, and West Philadelphia. In Tijuana we were in a gated compound unable to leave at night because we might get kidnapped, shot, and raped- in that order. In Philadelphia we weren't allowed to leave the house because we might get kidnapped, shot, and raped, in that order. Despite all the horrible things going on around me, I remained blissfully ignorant.

    When I was in third grade, my parents bribed my sister and I into going to Tijuana by promising to take us to Disneyland and California Adventures afterwards. All I ever wanted was someone to play with and that wish was granted. In Tijuana I connected with a local youngster, Bomarro, over my lego sets and green athletic Nike watch. We didn't speak the same language, but we spent nearly every day together frolicking in the dust and dirt as if we didn't originate from opposite sides of life. By the end of the trip I wanted nothing else but to stay with all the new friends from the city and the high school youth. In the departing van I wept for hours after we separated from the group. The same van that my parents kept reassuring me was taking us to Disneyland. How often do you hear of a kid weeping on the way to Disneyland?

    In Dominican Republic, my parents took my sister and I to shanty towns with small huts made of scrap metal; the kind of place that makes Skid Row look like Beverly

Hills. The children were fat with malnutrition and had rotten teeth from all the local sugarcane. I bet it's worth it, though- that shit was delicious. Sewage and other miscellaneous waste flooded the streets where children ran barefoot. Despite the putrid conditions, the only thing on my mind was "Can I play with the kids and can I pet that dog with saggy nipples?" No, no you cannot; both of them have diseases. Those naked children would run up to us, cheer at our blonde hair, follow us around, and freak out over the pictures being taken. They were so happy yet they had so little. I don't know why we went to those villages because they weren't the ones we were helping but it sure was enlightening. These experiences were important to my parents and now to me.

    One of our popular destinations was Rocky Mountain National Park, where my dad used to work at the YMCA when we was in college. We weren't one of those pussy campers with big motorhomes and televisions; we were real, tent-dwelling, mat-sleeping, rustic campers, living on the edge with a Gameboy and no extra batteries. We had one large tent for the four of us and cooked all our meals over the fire or propane camping grills. By we, I mean my dad did all the cooking. We would spend most of our time in the campground where we could swim in the piss warm pool, play mini golf, and handle the pet snake Cornelius at the the visitors center.

    Occasionally we would stray from the campground and venture into the wilderness. My parents never made me carry anything because they said they wanted us to enjoy the experience without thinking about the burdens on our back. That's a metaphor for childhood if I ever saw one. Our camp was set near the top of Adams Falls, where we built a fire and wandered aimlessly. At night we would play Pass the Pigs: a game where- instead of dice- you roll two little plastic pigs and the score was determined on how they landed. A stupid game, but tradition nonetheless and it was always anticipated with cheer and glee. Afterwards we would succumb to the soft sounds of the falling water and drift into a carefree slumber.

    One trip did not go so well. My dad took us to Utah where we were planning to do a three day hike through Fish and Owl Canyon Creek. This was when I was in fifth grade. The days were spent drenched in sweat and filled with dreams of soft beds and air conditioned hotel rooms. For this trip, I actually had to carry a pack filled with apathy and dread. Also food. A few pounds gets very heavy, very quickly when you're walking in the desert. Halfway along the required route was a fork in the road at which we had to keep left. If we went right, it would add three days to the loop, which we were not prepared for. We were moving at such a fast pace my dad didn't think we were at the fork, when indeed we were. So we kept right; the opposite direction of correct. We trekked half a day the wrong way and eventually my dad was getting confused because we were supposed to be by a creek the entire time, allowing us to have sufficient water. But there was only dust and sage bush, the smell of which haunts me to this day.

    There was supposed to be rivers all along this trail but there were none and we were running dangerously low on water. After my dad's latent spidey senses kicked in, he decided to scout ahead before we committed to a further distance. *I'm going to die in this stupid desert, aren't I?* An hour or so later he came back and we decided to be safe and go back home the way we came. We had no water but due to the gracious blessings of Mother Earth, we found some puddles caked with algae. We slipped the filter through, pumped what little moisture we could from the wet green goo, and tossed some iodine tablets in for good measure. It tasted like green diarrhea but was hydrating and I'm alive to tell the tale. We made it to a little oasis we had found along the way and camped there for the last fateful night. Eventually we made it back to the mini van all burnt and blistered. Sometimes you need extra motivation to get you out of sticky situations and sometimes that motivation is necessity and fear for your life.

 Every winter we would go sledding at the same hill but one day ended in a cold catastrophe. This day was a beautiful sledding day with children laughing, playing and frolicking through the snow with their tongues protruding from their chubby cheeks. After repeatedly and respectively descending and ascending the hill, we went exploring in the woods. We found some ice down by the river and, being the genius that I am, I decided to chunk off the ice on the edge. You know, where ice cold water is. Well, I fell in. It was cold. Adrenaline was coursing while Bre was screaming and trying to pull me up without success, so my dad had to rush to pull me out. I fell in up to my neck so my whole body and snow gear was completely saturated with freezing water. Despite my pleading to get a toe in the red sled, my dad forced me to walk up the hill back to the car. At the time, I though I was going to die from the frigid hike, but maintaining movement was what kept me alive. I'm no scientist, but hypothermia is worse than a short walk. Plus I got hot chocolate when I got home. Or Hot Pudding as my mom would call it because I dumped in way too much of that delicious chocolate cocaine powder. Which I will still eat by the spoonful.

*Dad's Letter*
*Wednesday May 28, 2008*
*Dear Toph,*
 *I happened to read something today in a book about*

the father and son that started the business of IBM. It was written by the son who often wrote about how much he and his dad fought. He said the would argue about once a month but always made up because he knew his dad loved him and that he loved his dad. He thought they argued because, as he put it,, "No son can ever do a good enough job for his dad. Wow! That made me think, "Does Toph think that way too?" Then I started thinking about different things that might make you think that you could never do a good enough job for me. I first thought of when you started mowing the lawn. I would get frustrated with you for missing strips un-mowed in the grass here and there. You didn't understand what the big deal was. Now I think you would understand that a little more that it makes it look nicer but I laugh now because I remember that you needed glasses so bad that you probably couldn't see the difference. When you could actually see, and got a little practiced, you did a good job.

 I never got to work with my dad when I was an adult but I never realized how much of an encourager he was until I worked somewhere other than the farm while I was growing up. Once I did that I remember talking to Uncle Keith about what that was like. Both of us agreed that in some ways it really sucked because nobody encouraged you and let you know that you were good at something. I think you realize how gifted you are with smarts. Since you are in advanced classes that may be obvious. However, the fact that you are so self disciplined when it comes to school work would not be so obvious with everyone. That can say more good about someone than just being smart. You have two big things going for you so I hope that gives you a ton of confidence.

 With all those things going for you I am proud of you for them but I'm more proud of you for having your *priorities right. Keith said you were excited about going on a service project with Harderwyk this summer. That is great, good for you! I think that type of thing is just part of who Christopher Paul DeKleine is. You, like your sister, are blessed so you turn around and bless others when you can.*

*Keith brought tears to my eyes last Sunday when he told me that you came and asked for envelopes to put your money into for different things. I was not surprised at how responsible you are but it made me feel good about myself a little bit because I remember sitting you and Bre down in the living room at age four and six and explaining the money envelopes to you. That money was what you got for cleaning your rooms. You could not wait to spend most of your money on Pokemon Cards, Bionicles and a bunch of other stuff but your long term savings added up to several hundred dollars after a while. As males, we get into the feeling "secure" with some money in the bank. You should feel good about yourself because you earned it.*

*You can do a lot of things and are smart but remember through it all that God loves you no matter what you can or can't do, what you've done or didn't do, and it doesn't make any difference how hard you work. I have a lot of guys around me that were not blessed as much as you and I were. I have to remember that God loves me and them too.*

*I hate to sound so preachy in these letters. Who am I to be giving advise or what is my encouragement worth you may be thinking. Well first of all I just write to try to let you know that I love you. Secondly, I want to let you know that you deserve to be loved. Not just by me but by so many other people as well. I hope you know that and feel that.*

*I'll end this letter- finally. I love you Bud.*
*Dad*

# Chapter 2: Murder Precursor

*Mom's Journal*
*April 4, 2007*
*"I am not a loser!!" She cried with her arms stretched skyward, palms wide open, fingers fanned apart, head tilted toward heaven.*
*"I AM NOT A LOSER!" She began to choke with tears of relief, of deep joy, of mourning. With her eyes closed, face to face with heaven, she felt the warmth of the sun glowing on her presences, his joy.*
*"Count it all joy; count it all joy." She felt it lifting her like a butterfly lighting from one flowered bush to another.*
*She knew beyond a shadow of a doubt that what she once was, by no cognizant choice of her own, could and would be no more. Her innermost person was being restored at last. She always knew that her real person, the person she knew a long time ago- the one who found energy and excitement in everyday, the one who was smart and witty, bubbly and bold, the one who over time began to crave the laughter of her youth, who became bonded to one who bullied and belittled, who over time slowly and blindly became a near nothing, a non-exist. A nobody, just a nobody. And try as she might, each time she felt her tiny bubble of self being chased seem helpless, happiness began to emerge. He was there with his pin, poking at her until she had no choice but to pop. What a loser.*

**Chapter 2 The Murder Precursor**

Side A: My Mother

Considering she is dead, I can no longer get her side of the story and a lot of the things she did were unknown, even to her closest friends. However, I will do my best with the information I have been given from family witnesses and the recollection of personal experiences. The especially juicy things have been verified by multiple sources who were there for everything. My father told me a few things and even though I trust him, they were verified by experience and various sources. Offense is not the intent to any of her close relatives, but the truth is truth. She's my mom and I have to deal with it too.

My mom grew up in a very ridged home, according to her. She told me that her father, my grandfather, wasn't a very loving person and never actually said the words, "I love you" to her, at least until later in life. Her words, not mine. My grandparents showed me nothing but love, which is why I am skeptical of her opinion. My mother never had a great relationship with her sister either, at least until just before her demise. They were constantly fighting for attention and resentment raised between the two of them, even as adults. They barely spoke in the years leading to the murder. Near the end, they began to reconnect and rebuild their relationship and had a heart to heart on Christmas, just fifteen days before the incident. I don't know what was said but both my aunt and my mom considered themselves best of friends afterwards and amends were made. Great timing, right? My mom was expressively happy about their newfound sisterhood after Christmas. At the hearing, my aunt said in her impact statement, "We had reconciled literally a year ago. We were connecting and becoming friends. Years of misunderstandings were being sorted through and I actually, after so many years of disliking her, told her I loved her on Christmas day. The last time I saw her alive."

Now, I don't want to paint a complete picture of my mom being a suicidal psychopath because that is not what she was completely. She was my the closest person in my life and we had many beautiful moments together and these moments are an important addition to the painting of crazy. Through pain and sadness, she always managed to have sense of humor. On one of our Church's Dominican Republic mission trips, she managed to misstep off a ledge, fractured her ankle and had to get a cast up past her patella. Maybe it was the pain killers, maybe it was her strong jovial attitude, but the rest of the trip contrived of joke after joke about the misfortune of her busted leg and the extremely anticlimactic scenario that caused it to be so. One night, the whole group got together to do some sort of comedy show consisting of people dividing into small groups to see who could come up with the best story of how the leg was broken because the real story was so boring. I will never forget the image of my mom sitting in the front row, with her leg up and a constant smile with outbursts of laughter. The winning story ended up being about a cockroach, La Cucaracha, crawling around the room while she swung at it with a cast iron frying pan. After scurrying around the kitchen, La Cucaracha climbed up her left leg and without realization gave one final deathly blow to the cockroach on her leg. That is the story of how she broke her leg in the Dominican Republic.

*Mom's Journal*
*May 9, 2007*
*I remember*

*Sitting on my mom's lap*
*Snuggling close in her embrace*
*Her look of approval and love*
*Her expression that I'd better shape up*

*I remember*
*Her daily phone calls with Mary Jo*
*With all those "m-hms" "ya's" and "oh's"*
*That meant she was listening*

*I remember*
*My mom making coffee and toast*
*Every morning for my dad*
*Before he gave her a quick peck*
*As he left for work daily*

*I remember*
*The smell of Comet Cleanser*
*And Spic-n-Span*
*Of Windex and Pledge*
*As my mother diligently cleaned our home*

*I remember*
*The meals she made for the four of us*
*She made meatloaf and chicken*
*Spaghetti and goulash,*
*Liver and onions, potatoes baked or mashed*
*The coho or lake trout or salmon on Sundays*
*Freshly caught by my dad the day before*
*Pizza on Sunday nights with a thick fluffy crust*
*Saturday meant hotdogs or hamburgers- something outside*
*A picnic when skiing on a weeknight away*

*I don't remember*
*Hugs from my dad*
*Or kisses on my face from him*

*I don't remember*
*The words "I love you"*
*Escaping from his heart and lips*

*I don't remember*
*Words of encouragement*
*Or of a job well done*

*I don't remember*
*Him coming to my sporting events*

*I don't remember*
*Ever finding it anything less than*
*Challenging to find my dad cards for holidays*

*I don't remember*
*Him comforting me in my childhood mishaps*
*Or times when I was sick*

*I don't remember*
*Dad telling me how much Jesus loved me*
*Or why we went to church or*
*Did devotions at supper every night*
*Or why he always said the same*
*Prayer at meals*

*I don't remember*
*Squealing with glee as my daddy*
*Pushed me in a swing*
*Or threw me in the air*

*Or tossed me into the lake for fun*

*I don't remember*
*Dad expressing his pride in me as*
*I brought home good grades*
*And good friends*
*And sang about Jesus*

*Thoughts of my mom will always be near*
*Time with Dad is becoming more dear*

Talk about daddy issues. Okay, I will thank you. I hate leaving that journal entry in the book because I love my grandpa so much and loathe how she felt about him. He's not an expressive individual, get over it. Did he put a roof over your head? Did he work to provide the food? Did he send you to a great private school? Love is an act just as much as it is a verbal expression. Love you and got your back gramps. She was spoiled and didn't even know it.

She blamed a lot of her problems on her parents and my dad. She left two notes at one of her suicide attempts; the one where she left the car running in the garage, or maybe it was the pills, or perhaps the gun, surely it must be the cutting one.. Let me sort through the pile of faulty attempts, nope it was the garage one. One of the notes was to my father, which was long, apologetic and full of love. The other she left to her parents, which merely said, "Good bye."

As an adult, blaming your parents for your own problems is infantile, mentally ill, incredibly self centered, or you're plain old ungrateful. Probably all four. Because where does the blame game stop? If you blame your parents for your problems, then they have the right to blame their parents and so on and so forth. Everyone has problems and issues. Own them. Playing the infinite blame game is useless. Once you become a conscious human person at whatever age and you realize your flaws, it is completely your responsibility to correct the errors or love them.

*From Dad,*
*I just finished reading mom's journal dated March 16, 2007. It reminded me of something her Psychiatrist told me right after he told me his diagnosis of her was Borderline Personality Disorder (BPD), but of course he could not tell her that. He warned me to be prepared for the eventuality of if I went against her in any way since it is typical for people with BPD to lash out viciously and with loathing toward anyone who goes against them. He said that, just like I had been experienced several times before, that she may tell you to do something, or that she is fine with me doing something I want to do, but then be furious when I do it. He referred to mom's reaction to my going to Iraq as Abandonment Rage and said even though she told me she was excited about me being able to go to Iraq and was supportive of me, after I left and came back, she did exactly what a typical BPD would do. She did a 180 degree turn and was spiteful of me for doing just what she said she supported me doing. He advised me to be prepared to go through hell from mom because BPD's have no gray areas and see nobody as in between good and bad. BPD's are either infatuated with someone or if they feel rejected by them, they rage against them. NO KIDDING! That's why she hated the pastor toward last. Rereading some of her emails about him, she changed from hanging on his every word like she did back in 1999 to loathing him too.*

Lori suffered from psychological disorders and stress

all her life, having been officially diagnosed with Bipolar, Borderline Personality Disorder and ADHD. Depression was something that has run in the family starting with my great-grandmother, then with my mother. At times, I was able to convince myself I had it, but realized I was just doing it to justify my lethargy and saw it more of a plea for attention. I am not saying that's what other people are doing but I do know it is what I was doing. Depression can be real; seek help, pray, meditate, find your distraction from the impending existential doom; do what you have to do to not hate yourself. In my opinion people are going overboard with diagnosing any social abnormality as a mental illness. This makes it easier to deal with and labeling can lead to reading into behaviors too much which in turn leads to self-fulfilling prophesies. Not to mention it too easily eschews the responsibility of one's actions when they can so easily cry themselves a victim of some disorder. "Oh man, I can't do X because I have Y." So get better at it by practicing and immersing yourself, that's how life works dingus. How about instead of pumping your brain full of bullshit chemicals, we try and change the physical world around us. If your job depresses you, get a new one. If you find yourself disliking your friends, get new ones. Feeling drowsy all the time, eat better and drink more water. Too much energy to sit still in school, go get some exercise then. It's not hard you are just weak-willed which isn't that big of a deal and completely fixable. I've done all these many times and I'm a sad sack lazy bastard.

  My mother had attempted suicide many times. Oh so many times. One time my father arrived home and received a call from one of my mom's coworkers who was a little worried and asked him if he knew where his gun was. He said yes and proceeded to verify, but it was not in the locked gun case buried in his dresser where it was supposed to be and proper gun safety dictated. He knew immediately where she would go, so off to the beach he went.

They ended up seeing each other on the road and met up back home. Following this attempt, she checked into the local psychiatric facility. It's the type of place they don't allow phone chords or plastic knives so you can't seppuku. Electro-shock therapy was used on her twice. At first this shocked me... pun intended. But it's not like the movies depict it: with the mouth rubber and screaming eyes. She was sedated and in an incredibly controlled environment. However, these days doctors don't use this method unless it is extreme circumstances which goes to show how crazy my mother actually was. Although after this happened, she was a shadow of her self for a couple months but would always recuperate.

She was found twice with knives, but only once with cuts on her arms. The other time she was sent to a facility was when my father found her in the garage with the car running. He said he got home from work and saw there were tool cases blocking the garage door and the second he walked into the house he smelled fumes. There he said he saw a vodka bottle and a glass sitting next to notes addressed to Ken, Mom and Dad, and her sister.

She attempted to overdose on pills- probably an SSRI or Benzo- once but failed. My dad wrote about finding her in the pill induced delirium: *I tried talking to her but she was quite incoherent and most of what she was trying to say was gibberish, nonsensical words and nothing made sense. Something she kept repeating was, "Seven, God's number. Seven, God's number, Seven, God's number." Later I found out she was trying to say she had taken seven of each of her medications because that was God's number of completeness. [Mom's Coworker] and I didn't know it at the time but mom was never in any danger of dying and her stomach contents confirmed that.*

For someone who wants to kill themselves so badly, she was awful at it. She went back to the clinic again after this episode. She was there for a week while my dad worked and visited her and my sister and I lived in blissful ignorance with my aunt and uncle- the same ones who took us in after the murder. My mother had been to many different doctors and therapists while ingesting many different medications. She was on and off pills, sometimes by her own volition, which any doctor will say is a big mistake.

Because "research on Borderline Personality Disorder is in it's early stages," according the The National Institute of Mental Health, it can "often be misdiagnosed as Bipolar." NIMH goes on saying those with BDP suffer from "Problems regulating emotions and thoughts, impulsive and reckless behavior, and unstable relationships with other people." They also have high rates of "concurring disorders such as depression, anxiety disorders, extreme reactions, a pattern of intense and stormy relationships, and recurring suicidal behaviors or threats." I witnessed her suffer from every single one of those. Psychology Today says sufferers of BDP are "often described as 'drama queens' or 'abusive'. They frequently create chaos in a situation where others would smoothly deal with normal differences and disappointments that arise from time to time for all of us."

My father said he was warned by her psychiatrist about Borderline Personality Disorder and he should watch out for signs of manipulation. Dr. Heitler in Psychology Today says, "There may well be some individuals with BPD who are genuinely manipulative or sadistic" but also goes on to say, "BPD sufferers get further stigmatized this way, that is, when clinicians label behaviors that stem from hyperemotional responsively with the pejorative term *manipulative*."

An article in the local news wrote she said Ken forced her to do sexual acts. Considering what I know about my father and the facts she construed, this is something I can't believe. He denies it and she's a bonafide liar. She also said he forced her into working at a Christian kids camp in California, at the beginning of their relationship. Here she found her first second love, marking the first time she cheated on him. My mom once told me about this experience and how she was traumatized by being forced into something against her will and this wouldn't have been the first time she agreed to something then immediately regretted it. But there's no way working out in California can be considered tragic. Not to mention, my dad made me do a lot of things out of my comfort zone too. The idea would often make me nervous, but then I'd carry through on it and literally every time I would end up admitting to my father it was a good choice. It's good to get out of your comfort zone and California is hardly that. Like NIMH said: "making mountains out of molehills is a common symptom of BDP."

The first time I saw my mother's depression was when I was maybe four or five. I walked into her bedroom and found her sitting on her bed weeping into her hands. The cause was unknown to me so I asked about the tears, but the only response I got was more sobbing. I tried to comfort her by putting on a bunch of her hats and making funny faces, but obviously those wouldn't help clinical depression.

My dad knew she was far gone and beyond repair but he was in balls deep at this point, having kids and all. Despite being right about her psychoses, he did not understand her illness or the proper remedies to take. He said he would call home from work frequently when he knew it was just her, my sister and I to make sure we were alive and not drowned in the bath tub or something. He also checked in with people she worked with just in case they were noticing anything odd about her. I was even told by family when everyone found out my mom was pregnant with Bre, everyone started praying real hard, which is West Michigan Christian for "This is fucked." Someone once told me, "When they were good, they were good, but when they were bad..."

Every kid used to fake being sick, but a couple times I didn't even have to. When I was in third grade there were a couple days where I was actually sick with the flu: puking, diarrhea, the lot of it. On the Friday of the week where fluids where exploding from damn near every orifice, I felt good enough to go to school, but that doesn't mean I actually wanted to. My mom asked me if I was good enough, to which I replied, "Probably" with a unenthusiastic gloom. She just looked at me, thought a minute and told me I can just stay home. It was Friday, she had the day off, and I was in third grade, how important could a few days learning how to add numbers or color or something actually be so she called the school and told them I wouldn't be attending for one more day. We took the day off and hung out just the two of us. We strapped on our snow gear and played and ran in the mounds of snow in the parking lot across the street proceeded by watching Back to the Future II on our thirteen-inch TV and drinking hot chocolate on the couch. Of course there were many days she would call me out on my bull shit and send me to school like a good parent, but these momentary gems shine bright and these are the memories I chose to focus on.

When I was in seventh grade, my mom finally found a therapist to be enthusiastic about- we'll call him John

Doe. She heard about him through a friend that sang his praises after they'd been seeing him. If she reads this, I really hope she doesn't feel responsible for what happened. She became infatuated with many people over the years and this wasn't an isolated event. It wasn't long before she was singing the same song she always did. At the time, I was happy, she was happy and so was my dad.

We refurbished the kitchen and had plans to redo the bathroom because of all the sweet military dough my dad was raking in. Money stress was alleviated for a while and life felt lighter, despite my dad not being home. But the train wasn't filled with just gravy.

While my dad was in Iraq, and my mother visiting the new therapist, the relationship between her and John grew like a tumor. My mother and her therapist started hanging out far beyond the boundaries a psychologist and patient should. Strangers that read more about this said on internet forums he closed the patient file on her before this happened, meaning he was doing it pro-bono and she wasn't a technical- on paper- patient. She ended up going to his house all the time to either hang out with him, his wife, or his entire family. I even went a few times and I'm not gonna lie, it was fun at the time. John had an awesome CD collection and even let me borrow a few of the classics. I learned a lot about music from this guy although I can't listen to The Eagles or Tom Petty without thinking about him. So says The Dude, "I hate the fucking Eagles, man." His family was pretty cool and we would watch movies and they would play music. I was bigger than his boys, so we would wrestle and I would win. Despite my enjoyment, this relationship was wrong. Strangers on that same forum say John found his second wife while he was therapizing her during *her* first marriage. Allegedly he had attempted to seduce multiple patients as well.

My dad once asked my mom why she was going over to John Doe's all the time. He said she replied, "Yesterday, their daughter (about five or six) grabbed my face between her hands and looked me in the eyes and said, 'Mrs. DeKleine, I love you.' I don't get that from my kids at home so why would I go there?" We were teenagers, of course we weren't going to do that. She chose to have us, we did not choose to have her. Plus it's not like she was putting any amount of effort into our relationship either. The only words that came out of her mouth for a long while were complaints about my father. I get it, though. I didn't want to go home because I didn't feel like I was enjoyed or loved, so why be there? A familial failure on both our parts.

Lori was showing mischievous signs while my dad was away in Iraq. She told him that the three of us- her, my sister and I- wanted him to extend his stay for another year. I said no such thing and do not recall ever being asked such a question. When my dad got home from Iraq, he knew things weren't right. He suspected an affair and sought evidence in many different ways. He said in a letter he never found the "smoking gun." After being home a few months something happened: a heated conversation that ended with my mom sleeping on the couch. I asked my dad about this conversation, but he doesn't remember what was said. She didn't sleep in the same bed with him ever again.

It turns out this relationship between my mom and her therapist wasn't the first love affair she had thrown herself into. The first one being before they got married, the one in California. I don't know what happened but I do know that when confronted by multiple people about it, she never denied anything, but also never accepted blame. I was also told she had a fling that got "too serious" before she was in this relationship, which means she had pre-marital coitus/banged some dude.

After my father's return from Iraq, they went rolling on a relationship rollercoaster. Sometimes things seemed like they were getting better while other times they got worse. The next summer we had a family meeting at the dinner table. My mom said things were getting better and she was working on forgiving my dad for whatever he did. My sister started talking about how this was an answer to prayer and she had feared a divorce. My father admitted to being wrong about a few things but said they both had some stuff to work on yet. *Sweet! things are looking up.*

Then came the divorce talk. That was in October of 2006, during my freshman year. My parents sat us down at the same dinner table and made the announcement. I handled it better than my sister, who stormed off downstairs and wept for a while. I just sat there in disgust until my dad said that I should probably go comfort her. So I did what I could. My sister sat sobbing on my chair- my happy place where I used to watch *The Simpsons* while fervidly consuming Little Debbie Honey Buns and Nutter Butters. There I sat hugging her head and reminiscing about sweet treats while she sobbed.

After the divorce talk, they still lived in the same house for a while. Eventually my mother migrated to the basement where she turned our old workout room, my Simpsons and Honeybun room, into her second bedroom. This was incredibly awkward when having friends over because the basement was "sleep over place" and my friends and I would hang out there all night while my mom went into a benzo coma in the room next door and my dad upstairs. Not an easy situation to explain. It made me pretty choosey with whom I invited over and limited my social life greatly.

From there things got worse. One point my dad tried to break into her room. He was an idiot, broke the window and cut himself, leaving blood stains on the floor. She then seized the opportunity to take pictures to use as evidence to file a Personal Protection Order against him and he was no longer aloud in his own house. I remember stumbling upon those pictures on our family computer with disgust and disappointment in the both of them.

    My mother never spoke well of my father. She would frequently complain about her problems and husband's antics. I listened and agreed far too much at first, but eventually grew exhausted from the whole situation and rarely returned home before bed. Her hatred for my father was obvious so whenever I had a beef with him, she was the one I went to for affirmation. I even told her about the unexplained loathing I had for my father throughout my entire life, with which she agreed and fueled. Even after the screwdriver-hockey debacle, I talked to her about how pissed off I was. She then started talking about how angry my father was and how controlling he can be, which, with hindsight, just wasn't the case.

    I eventually started to see through some of the bullshit and began to back off. I remember telling my sister, right after the murder, that I was glad she died when she did because I felt the relationship slipping. It was an "at least we left on a semi-positive note" type thing. After I grew tired of their egotistic escapades, I stopped going over to John Doe's with her, talked to her a whole lot less, and began finding other things to do other than be home.

    Hanging out with my friends was a great escape and I made sure to tell them that. To my high school friends, I would like to say thank you. You never made me feel weird about saying the depressing stuff and sometimes I took that for granted. One time, during the divorce process, my friends and I were at some church youth group event and the leader asked if anyone had anything on their mind. I felt compelled to express something. This was a weird compulsion because I am not a verbally expressive individual. It felt like every muscle in my body wanted to do it but my brain was holding me back. Well I couldn't resist anymore so I got up, took the microphone and told everyone how my friends had given me a home away from home and how happy they made me.

Since I stopped being home and talking to my mother, I really don't know a lot about what she did in the few months before the murder. I woke up one morning to get ready for school and she was there in her sweat pants, trying to keep my sister and I at a steady pace. Well, my sister at least; I was always punctual. I told her Bre was taking too long and we had to catch the carpool. She yelled at her to hurry up. I said good-bye. When I came home, her body was in the basement.

*Dad's Letter*
*Monday July 14, 2008*
*Dear Keith,*

*Wow, after last week I wish I could go back to just before the second time I came home from Iraq. Or, I kind of want to think that, "I wish I had not come back." To have kept things the way they were, in some ways, seems like it might be better. But that's not the way it works. Time marched on, and now I find myself and a lot of people in a very different situation. It would be easy to think that I wish I had never come back from Iraq. I started to think that just before I started writing this letter. Then, "Focus on the Family" came on and I heard just what I need to hear. "I can still have significance wherever I end up" was the message I got out of it.*

*[Brother] said you were planning on coming this last*

*weekend until you found water in your basement again. Good grief! That is the last thing you needed. I hope there was not too much damage. That sucked in 2007 for you guys when that happened.*

*That makes me wonder what Bre and Toph's rooms are like. I can imagine all kinds of stuff all over the floor. Bre can live like that always and Toph can do it for a while but then he has to clean it up every once in a while. [Nephew] said Toph's headboard was done and it's in his room. I bet he likes that.*

*It sure was great to see Toph. He looked so great and seems so much more confident. What a good kid he has always been and I'm sure he will continue to be. Seeing his head of hair made me wonder how many girls like running their fingers through his hair. I can imagine him saying it bugs him but really he loves it.*

*You will have been to the Calvin orientation by the time you get this. I hope that all went well. I would think they do a pretty good job of making you feel welcomed and well informed. Don't plan on Bre communicating too well about things you need to know. She is gifted in other ways.*

*How are you doing Keith? How is Jan doing? I appreciate your being at the trial everyday but I'm sure that it was not easy. Especially testifying. In some ways I wanted to testify but there was no way I could keep it together and not be a blubbering mess. you did very well and must have felt a lot of prayers supporting you. I know I was.*

*I continue to process everything. I miss Bre and Toph so much at times. I could let that eat me up but I've learned to turn these times into a time of prayer. That has enabled me to lift them up to God like never before. Maybe some people, including Bre and Toph, can't put much stock in my saying that yet but I hope they see that and feel that some*

*day.*
*Give my love to Bre, Toph and everyone else.*
*Love Kennyman*

Side B: My Father

    My father grew up on the DeKleine Family chicken farm in Drenthe, Michigan. He used to tell me stories about the bed him and his siblings would all share to keep warm in the vicious winter months. The house was so old, wind and snow would sneak through the cracks and create drifts in the house. There was one snow storm that laid snow so thick he got lost on the way to the barn, so everyone had to go searching for him. I still get to hear these stories from my uncle, which I enjoy every time. There is also a hilarious picture of Bre on the chicken farm when she was about two. It was during slaughtering day so there are a bunch of chickens hanging upside down without their heads and blood dripping to the ground. My dad is standing beside her with a shit-eating grin and toddler Bre is sitting, staring at the carcasses, and bawling her eyes out. Chicken life.
    Because of life on the farm, he used a lot of tough love. He frequently had that gruff "suck it up, build some character" type of attitude when I would complain but have since come to appreciate. When we would hike in Colorado, I would constantly ask how long we would have left to hike, to which he would reply, "How Long is Chinese." It's about the journey, not the destination, man.
    When I was young, maybe fifth or sixth grade, I came up with the idea to mow the lawn for a measly fee of five dollars. After I did it once, I was suddenly the lawn mower of the family and was expected to do it for the rest of my childhood. Well, I kept doing it and my father noticed I was

missing a few spots and leaving tall grass streaks in the lawn. So he took me out one day to show me my mistakes. I assumed he was belittling me so I took it personally and used that brick in building my house of resentment. I didn't understand because of general apathy towards modern lawn care as well as I physically couldn't see my mistakes. My father noticed my confusion and took me to get my balls checked. Eye balls. For some reason I thought getting glasses would be cool, so I actually got excited. Turns out my vision was pretty bad.

    Dad was all excited to take me to the eye doctor because he knew it would be a huge difference in my ability to function as a human being. Boy was he was right. After the appointment and donning of the glasses, I was blown away by the detail reality actually contained. On the way home I kept taking my glasses on and off to compare my sight. I would read aloud all the signs and words I could suddenly see so clearly. It was a revelation. He just sat back and smiled and probably said "I told you so" a few times. I eventually got a headache because of the all the on-off. No regrets.

    Because of the unexplained loathing I had for him, the conversation in which my dad revealed his departure for Iraq was oddly relieving. But at the same time I felt pride for him. It was an exciting change and in a selfish way, I was glad to be able to say my dad was going to Iraq to do some good. America. Also, I would have a bit more freedom on the home front. The conversation was at that fateful dinner table after him and my mom had both decided it was okay for him to go. They both affirmed to my sister and I that if we had any reservations, they would put a kibosh on the process. Bre and I agreed it was cool.

    His duty was to train prospective Iraqi police officers to be the best cops possible. It was only a year and he'd be making double what he did at the department and would also be able to visit twice for a couple weeks at a time. We ended up having a going away party at a local coffee shop where people gathered and donated some money to the family. Although my parents ended up giving it all to charity because we didn't need it and he was going to be making the big bucks slaying muzzies in the desert.

The whole dad-in-Iraq thing was all over the papers. Our family was interviewed, put in the news and papers, giving us a little bit of fame in West Michigan. Both parents stayed pretty humble throughout this whole thing although I know they both enjoyed it; we all did. We got a float in the Tulip Time Parade even though I was already marching in the school band with my saxophone, literally the sexiest instrument on the planet. My principal at school had me stand up in the middle of an assembly to say how proud he was of me and my attitude during the whole situation. That was awkward. I just stood up, flashed the peace sign then sat back down. Friggin' hippie.

The year my father was in Iraq I became much more independent and started cooking my own meals and washing my own clothes. Things a parent should probably have been doing. The only reason I started doing this was because no one else was doing it for me. I wasn't happy with the meals I was getting and my laundry would sit there for way too long and control freak me just can't handle that situation. This was around the time I also started to avoid being at home. It was more often than not that we had a "free for all" at dinner time and the remaining family began to give up on being together. My mom started hanging out with John Doe and my sister could have been slinging dope for all I knew. That's what theater kids do, right?

You don't know what you got 'till it's gone, so I began to appreciate my father in his absence and realized how much he held the family together. I genuinely missed him and liked it when he called. This one time I was allowed to take my mom's cell phone into class on my birthday because he was going to call to give me some well wishes. I missed the first one because I didn't want to interrupt the class but then left and hoped that he would be able to redial. The phone call finally came through and we spoke. I cried a little and told him I missed him after he wished me a happy birthday. After a brief and static-filled conversation, I closed the yellow and black, bumble bee, Nextel flip phone and skulked back into class.

    We were able to make the best of the times my dad came home. We mostly stayed in Holland and enjoyed each others presence trying to make it how it was before all this nonsense. My mother and him had a little vacation for themselves and stayed in a hotel for a couple nights abroad in the Netherlands, our motherland. I remember accidentally seeing a picture of her in lingerie when my dad was flipping through some of his photos and hastily went to the next one and said I wasn't supposed to see that. Nice. At the same time, we had become accustomed to life without him, so it took adjustment when he was home. Suddenly I couldn't do whatever I wanted and family dinner was expected.

    Another time when he was home, he was arriving just as one my soccer games kicked off. This was my eighth grade year, the season we went undefeated. I was playing forward and knew he was en route so made sure to keep my eyes peeled open for the white mini van to arrive. It pulled up in parking lot and I felt a rush of excitement. Just as he was in sight of the field, the ball was passed to me and I proceeded to drill it right into the back of the net. I looked up and there my dad was hooting and hollering; dad got to see me score a goal. My coach knew what was going on so he pulled me out of the game immediately so I could go see him- "KLEINEY GET OFF THE FIELD!" I ran as fast as I could and leaped full fledged right into his arms. I'm sure there were people ogling at the precious patriotic display, but I wasn't paying attention to them at all.

    It was many years until I learned just how horribly things in Iraq went for him. He was always one to keep busy and do his job above and beyond the call of duty so when he saw slackers he pointed them out. He wrote letters to the bosses at camp about people who weren't doing what they were getting payed to do and how much that ticked him off. Despite my father's honest intentions, he was threatened by one of his bosses that he would lose his $10,000 bonus: money that had already been spent to refurbish our kitchen. This was one of those points of tension he failed to communicate to my mother, who had no idea what was going and I'm sure that didn't help the relationship. I don't know what he did, but we still got the money.

    Apart from getting shot at next to a bunch of soldiers failing to do their job, he had some troubles with the locals. One day, when they were gathering recruits, he was asked what age the recruits should be from a town nearby. Using common sense, or thinking it was like the US, he said eighteen because that's the legal age for the draft. Apparently he was wrong and the age of requirement was actually twenty-one. About twenty young people, deemed too young, were brought to a base needlessly only to find out they can't be there and were subsequently bussed back. However, the bus was captured by insurgents on their way back and every single one of those kids was shot in the head. Talk about wrong place, wrong time. These were young men and women who wanted to help their country. They are dead because my dad made one faulty decision that was based on understandable logic. No wonder people come back from places like that all messed in the head.

A few months after he got home, the tension in the house started to rise. I recall one night when my dad took me to the church gym across the street to play some lacrosse and let off some steam. At one point he just sat down and let out a large sigh. I knew something was wrong based on the look of extreme exasperation on his face but since I didn't really care about him and just wanted to play some got-damn lacrosse, I didn't ask. He started talking anyway. He confessed to saying something awful to my mom and despite my situational apathy, I had a minor amount of pity for the bastard so I enabled further conversation. I asked what he said to her, but he refused to tell me. At one point he asked me, his eighth grade son, for advice. I told him that sometimes it's too difficult to take on the emotions of others and that looking out for yourself isn't always selfish. He said that was very wise advise although I was probably talking out of my ass per the usual.

It took about a year of him being home before my mom issued a Personal Protection Order against him. After the PPO was issued and he was kicked out of his house, things kept getting worse. He lived with my aunt and uncle for a while and started to see someone, unbeknownst to me. I met her once and didn't pay it any mind but apparently she was torn apart at the trial, even though she had nothing to do with the murder. The rule of my aunt and uncle's house is that you can't have a girl at home alone with you, something I also had to live by. But since he was an adult he didn't follow that rule and they would often see her coming down the road as they were leaving. He later admitted to having sex in the house, which was pretty upsetting to everyone else because he was still technically married although they had been separated for a very long time. All this despite the fact his wife had been cheating on him a long time already, kicked him out of the house, and alienated him from his children. I can't blame the guy for wanting to get some but our culture dictated that to be unsavory and promiscuous.

    My father was able to gather a decent amount of evidence against my mother while he was out of the house. He had gathered enough where he thought it to be a good idea to confront her with data in hopes of having a rational conversation but took a couple comrades with him to our house just in case things went awry. I was there with my mom at the cursed dinner table when they arrived and politely asked me to leave. Here three big dudes come into my house looking all sorts of confrontational and asked me to leave my mom alone. I refused. They tried to convince me more. I still refused. Finally my uncle kneeled beside, looked me dead in the eyes and said, "Christopher, I am here to make sure everything is okay and nothing happens to anyone, especially your mother. She will be safe." I looked into his eyes, believed him, and lethargically left my house. I don't remember where I went, probably my youth leader's house or a friend's. I didn't find out until much later what was said that night.

    I have spoken to all three of the men who went to confront my mother that fateful night. My father had conclusive data confirming her adulterous activities with John Doe. Not only did she have an affair with John, but engaged in lesbian activities with his wife. He also talked about all the other infatuations she had with other people throughout their marriage. Some of them even had to send her cease and desist letters or told my dad about their predicament. I'm not going to say who they were but it was about a half dozen people throughout the marriage. Some of the attempts succeeded, others did not. Allegedly she even tried to seduce our pastor. But he's a pastor and a stand up guy so thankfully nothing happened. John made an appearance to help defend her, but nothing ever came of that night besides a deeper shit hole and this paragraph.

When my dad was out of the house and I was in my freshman year, appendicitis struck my guts and I had to get it wretched out of my stomach. I was watching television at home alone and a sharp pain began to bite my lower right abdomen. I tried to convince myself it was extreme hunger or something else but I couldn't even stand up straight. It felt like my intestines were getting pulled out through a small hole and almost yelled "Freeeeedooooom" just for the sake of it. After giving up on the whole standing business, I knew something was wrong and medical care was a necessity. I called my mom's cellphone. She didn't pick up. I knew she was at John Doe's. I wasn't worried but I called again. Still nothing. I did this for a while, at least fifteen calls (I checked her phone afterwards) and was starting to panic. My dad was on duty and I didn't want him involved but the pain was so intense, I had to cave into this last resort and call him. He was there within a few minutes and had to break his PPO to come and get me out of the house.

After a few steps outside, I immediately vomited over the deck and my mom's Germanias, which were scarred from bile for years after. He took me to the hospital while I flinched with every bump in the road. The male nurse kept failing at finding a vein for the IV drip, but the pain was a new pain that took me away from the hot knife being stabbed into my gut so I was actually thankful he kept stabbing me.

My dad was with me the entire time while my mom showed up over a half hour late and in a panic. In situations like these, there's no point in trying to decipher what she was doing at the time; probably an intense game of Scrabble.

    The doctors made me drink a disgusting chalky liquid for my insides to appear on the CAT Scan so I deep throated the straw to avoid the taste and chugged it as quick as humanly possible. I had just read Roald Dahl's autobiography *Boy*, in which gets appendicitis and describes my painful experience to the T. I drew some conclusions and told my dad what I had on the way to the hospital so when the doctor came back and turned my suspicion into fact, my dad said he was impressed, but I didn't care, I was in pain. The surgeon cleaved me open early in the morning the next day. The rest of the day I slept and ingested whatever opioids I could, remaining barely conscious for my visitors. I hated my parents for the tangible tension they created by being in the same room. They hardly spoke to each other and sat on opposite sides of the room while I laid in my hospital bed all hopped up on Vicodin.

    My dad's lust for evidence and "the smoking gun" never stopped; he was obsessed. Like I said, he broke into the house and left blood stains. Not a good look on his part. This combined with some fallacies, my mom managed to trash his name in the community by saying he was an abuser. Although no one will ever know what happened but them, I have a hard time believing any abuse happened. In my childhood there were many moments where they would start tonguing each other after a conversation while Bre and I would sit there in hilarious disgust. There was love between them and we shouldn't forget it.

    My mother managed to get a lot of people on her side. Most of these people ended up being friends she had made while my dad was in Iraq. All new ones who didn't even know Ken before any of this. I remember wondering why so many new friends were popping into her life all of a sudden. A lot of their long term friends knew what was up to and sided with my dad, which didn't help at all. One other couple was caught in the fray of this shit-show. They had been having some marital issues as well and apparently my mom was encouraging the woman to divorce her husband. This angered my father even more, considering that was one of his best friends from college. Plus who is my mother to meddle in a relationship when she was obviously god-awful at her own.

Many people think Iraq was what made my father go crazy. I deny it; he denies it; his family denies it; his friends deny it. Despite certain tragedies, it's not like he was fighting commies in the shit. He was mainly in a camp training people away from the action. The lady he used to visit, Fay Key, who I will talk more about later, said he seemed weird after he got home but went on to say it was probably because of the deep and vast relationship issues, which is more likely. Other friends and family of his tell me Lori was all he talked about and all he could focus on after he came home. My uncle had to tell him to let it go and cool his jets but the jets were far from cooled.

One thing you think about as a kid when your parents are getting divorced is dual holidays. Double presents, yay! But being thrown into the middle of a breaking family makes holidays the least joyous time of the year. The first Christmas we had without him, my mother talked to me about whether or not she should let him come to our grandparent's house for the day. I told her I would rather have him not be there. On the Thanksgiving before my father took my sister and I to Cracker Barrel before we went to the other festivities. He kept talking about wanting to make this a tradition while playing one of those stupid peg board games and desperately attempting to spur on any conversation. We were not amused. I just kept looking at my mom's loaned bumble bee phone hoping my she would call so we could get out of there. That was the worst dinner of my life.

    My dad tried to bond with me all the time. He would pick up any interest I had and beat that horse past its expiration. After he moved out of my aunt and uncle's he was given a house to live in for a short time from a friend of his. It was pretty close to home so it was convenient for him but since he was by no means wealthy, the furniture was pretty sparse. He had a mattress on the floor for his room, a futon for me and my sister's room, and an old TV on the floor with a antique floral couch in the living room. In hopes of trying to get us to come over more often he bought a Nintendo Wii. He lied to us saying a friend bought it for him so my sister and I would have something to do at his house but I don't see why he thought it mattered who bought it. I just ignored him while playing the shit out of it and got really good at Wii boxing. I used to think the phase of not wanting to be around my parents was normal for any kid but it turns out lots of kids actually liked their parents. Huh.

    Apart from the blatant relationship issues, no one could foresee this murder thing happening. People in the news and on forums blame everyone from my family to his coworkers and boss about failing to foresee this insane scenario. This is the question that angers everyone in the family the most: "Did you see it coming?" Of course no one saw it fucking coming are you kidding me? If we did, we would have done something about it. And since when is the idea of murder on anyone's mind? My father was doing some pretty extreme and desperate things but kill her? He had filed with the state pointing out the unlawful relationship my mother had with her psychologist, but they were taking too long so he got impatient and felt forced to take things into his own hands- literally if the things are my mom's neck. I often wonder what would have happened if he had waited it out, but while he was sitting there, my mother was out convincing the public he was a sycophant and he was losing credibility by the day.

Eventually he grew impatient, frustrated, and irrational. He was correct up until the point he killed her. He was alone and what does any creature do when they are alone and feel backed into a corner? They resort to their final animalistic instinct, lash out and strangle their estranged wife.

*Until January 9, 2008 I was still holding out hope that mom would make a turn for the better. It was not to be.*

*Dad's Letter*
*Sunday August 17, 2008*
*Dear Keith,*

*It's been a while since I've written but I figured you were gone and the letters would just sit until you returned anyway.*

*Yes, I would like to stay up on everything the kids are doing. Talking to [friend] a few minutes ago he said that will be important for them down the road. He told me about a friend at work whose dad was in prison. That dad pretty much said that since he couldn't be in his kids' lives he didn't want to hear anything about them or have anything to do with them. That was really hard on the kids when their dad died in prison a while back. It would be easier for me in the same ways not to think about them at all but I don't want that. Whatever's best for them. Yes, I do love them very much.*

*You asked for some prayer requests. I guess one would be for my self image to keep improving. Now I'm realizing how much I was getting brought down by Lori and John for two years. First I started doubting myself and self worth so much. Then they started telling me how terrible I had been to Lori and the kids for twenty years. So a request would be for me to always know how much God loves me no matter what.*

*Next would be to assuage the sorrow I have of missing the kids and everybody. A prayer of thanks would be that I'm amazed at how much peace I have in all of this. I'm not worried about where I am going to any great extent. I'm pretty content.*

*Well I'll be looking forward to seeing you on the 23rd or 24th. Give my love to everyone for me.*

*Love Ken*

*Dad's Letter*
*January 26, 2008*
*Dear Jan and Keith,*

*Thank you again so very much. I will never be able to say that enough for what I have thrown upon you. Even knowing that I will keep saying it. I know the kids are in good hands and in some ways I know they are now even in better hands.*

*These Blessings for Bre and Toph are for them when they are ready for them. I realize it may be a long time and some times I think it may be never.*

*[He] and [Her] were here to visit today. [She] asked me how I was feeling and I told her it seems really strange about how I feel. Here I am in Jail, I will be going to prison for a long time or the rest of my life but I feel so free. FREE like I could never imagine. In a lot of ways I feel like I freed Bre and Topher too. I know this has done a lot of terrible things to them, I'm still having to face that. On the other hand, no more blackmail, no more extortion, no more*

*manipulation, and no more lying from Lori. For them, me, or anybody else. I think more things that Lori had up her sleeve will be coming out as time goes by.*

*I hope you get to start seeing Toph's funny side coming out soon if you have not already. I was worried about how he was sleeping a while back. Then I remembered that worrying about how he will sleep is what he stays awake worrying about. Once he adjusts he has always done fine with anything. I know this situation has been traumatic to say the least and is a lot for him to process but I think he will bring it to God and ask for His help. I know I have for him several times already. A better son I could not ask for.*

*Isn't Bre the Greatest! I have often though of Bre as being the best of your daughters, not that they have anything bad about them at all, but Bre just seems to be a mix of the both of them, the best parts.*

*I'm afraid to ask how MIFA is going, but how is it going? Living Hope? Showcase? Semi-formal? And the list goes on. She knows how to live life doesn't she? The amazing thing is that she was really having a shitty senior year but she tried to make the best of it. I think a lot of kids may have given up making the best of it by now.*

*A lot of people seem very concerned for me. I am doing fine as far as my attitude is going. I'm not bullshitting you either. I am completely safe, I sleep great, and the food is good and healthy. I am in my own little world but I have been blessed by God to have had forty-four years of so many BIG world experiences that I can remember. I can pass hours just laying on my mat thinking of all the opportunities I have had and the fact that I have been able to share so many of them with Bre and Toph. One regret Keith is that I never got to take you out West backpacking. Maybe Toph and Bre could do that someday.*

HA

*Why am I writing so freaking small? I have one little golf pencil to write with. It I write big like I normally would, by the time I was half way done, the pencil would be so dull it would be like reading a letter written with those huge crayon we had in kindergarten.*

*That's all for now. LUV YOU GUYS!*

*P.S. Could you send me that Christmas picture of the kids and me? 5x7 is the size limit and only five pictures per envelope. Also, if church could send the bulletin and the Banner to me here it would be great.*

# Chapter 3: 10 January, 2008

The first letter from my father deserves an individual introduction. This letter has been kept from many in my family because of its controversial nature. My dad never wanted people to see this, although I do have permission for full transparency. Because the letter was written right after the murder- 17 days- it gives an immediate and unapologetic glimpse. Reading this was crucial for me in taking a step of understanding and henceforth forgiveness.

It was written to one of his long term friends, whose name I have changed to protect his/her identity. For fear of libel and defamation suits, I have also changed the name of the nippledick therapist my mom cheated on him with, despite him being a twat. Even though he confessed, it's on public record, and you can Google our names to find the details anyway. Never found out what happened to him- other than a suspension- but I assume he is wallowing in his own excrement somewhere in the gutters of Calcutta.

Which reminds me of a neat journalistic trick used by many journalists called the "Small Penis Rule." From the New York Times, 1998: "For a portrait to be actionable, it must be so accurate that a reader of the book would have no problem linking the two," said Mr. Friedman. "Thus, he continued, libel lawyers have what is known as 'the small penis rule.' One way authors can protect themselves from libel suits is to say that a character has a small penis, Mr. Friedman said. 'Now no male is going to come forward and say, 'That character with a very small penis, that's me!'" Despite this loophole, I have drastically changed the fellow-with-a-small-penis's name to John Doe.

This was one of the first letters he wrote to anyone after being incarcerated and gives an incredibly solid view of how he felt before and after the murder. For the letter legend: Gomer is a prostitute in the Bible's book of Hosea. Also January 10, 2008 was when he killed her and he confessed on January 11.

*Dad's Letter*
*January 27, 2008*
*Dear [Friend],*
*Thank you so much for your kindness and friendship. Like I said to you over a year ago, "There are just some people that you know you can always go to and you know they will be accepting, caring, and loving." You are one of those people. I have seen you be that way with other people and now I have been experiencing it for myself. Thank you again.*

*Now to answer some of your questions. Yes I am safe. They have kept me completely separate from anyone else. I am OK with that and the guards always ask me how I am doing. Some are willing to talk a little bit. Someone from Mental Health comes by at least once a day to see if I need to talk to someone. They are very nice.*

*I am getting plenty of <u>sleep</u>. A lot of people ask me that and I understand why it is a concern, but I am at peace and have Shalom like I have not had in a long time. I can say I am sleeping better now than I have for over two years now. Looking back I was awake for hours at night while I was still in Iraq because I had started worrying about Gomer and [John Doe] (Gomer- read Hosea). Ever since January 11, 2008 I have been sleeping fine. I think you will understand better as you read further why I have such Peace.*

*<u>Visitors:</u> Yes I get a half hour visit once a week. My mom and brother came last week just before my mom went back to Florida. This week my sister and brother came on*

*Saturday morning.* I told my family to put you on the list to visit sometime. (I'd call you but I don't have your number). My brother is coordinating visits.

<u>Encouragement:</u> Yes I have gotten several letters of encouragement. I even got one from WOODTV8 saying that they would like to give me a chance to give and get my side of the story through them! HA! Yea right! No thanks.

It is great to hear about [Daughter]. Pictures would be awesome. 5x7 is the size limit and five per envelope. Hint. Hint. From what I hear Bre and Toph are doing well. They are living life and making the adjustment. I'm glad I had a chance to live with Jan and Keith for a while and see how fun loving and peaceful at the same time their house really is. I know in my heart that the kids are in a great home now. I know they have a lot of crap to process right now but I still think this is all turning out for the better. Bre and Toph are well loved, Lori is not suffering depression or whatever anymore and I am at peace knowing these things- along with the hope of still being used by God in some way.

I said I would explain why I am at such peace. Friend, here I am, sitting in prison, knowing that I may well spend the rest of my life here, but I feel so Free! I am not worried sick about what Gomer is doing to the kids anymore by her lies, manipulation, blackmail and extortion. I am FREE from worrying about what she is going to come up with next about me or anybody else. The extent she was willing to go to in order to protect her relationship with [John Doe] may never fully be known but I know I am FREE of that. Yes I hurt a lot of people and I know I did some incredible psychological damage to Bre and Toph but I still think they have an element of relief in them also. I think they were starting to catch on to some of her things but having grown up with it they may not realize a lot of what she was doing for a long time. I feel like- do *you remember back in 1975 when the Vietnamese were trying to get out of Vietnam? Parents were pushing their kids on to planes so they could get them out so the kids would not have to grow up under communist rule. Do you remember those images on TV? How painful the look on the faces of the parents and kids were. I feel like one of those parents. I tried, as well as everyone else did, to minimize the effects of Gomer on the kids and me but it was a losing battle. To FREE the kids and me (and other people as well) felt I had to "put them on a plane." It was/is painful but we are FREE! I could not "get on the same plane" as Bre and Toph so I may never get to see them again and they may never fully understand, hating me in some way for what I have done. However, I still feel... there is NO justification for what I did. People have asked me why I didn't ask for help. I did and I think everyone did what they could have. So many people tried talking to Gomer but that only seemed to make it worse. Her psychosis, excuses, illness, justification only increased. So, having to choose between what I thought was Yuck and Yuckier, I chose YUCK! I know this is arguable. Gomer's family would like to go a few rounds with me, but I hope someday this will be clearer to everyone. When at wits end and between a rock and a hard place, things get "weird."*

*I found out Friday that [John Doe] finally confessed to the detectives that he and Gomer had an affair. I have not been able to confirm this but it came from my lawyer. Talk about mixed feelings. I had still held out hope that Gomer had not stooped so low as to have an all out affair. She had had several infatuations with other men before but I don't know of any that went this far. On the other hand, it is nice to have validation to all my concerns and to know that all my suspicions were not from an abusive/controlling mind like she said I had. For [John Doe]- I kind of see him as another one of Gomer's victims. If not John so much, his wife and their three kids sure are. Of John and Gomer together we are all victims. I saw how Bre and Toph were victims long before I came back from Iraq. AM I VENTING OR WHAT? At least as my lawyer said, "He won't be able to do this with anyone else again." That is one good thing to come out of it.*

*Oh, you said in the first letter I got from you that you were sorry you didn't see this coming and thought maybe you had missed some hints. No I kept this completely to myself. I felt when it got to a certain point I would need to do this and I was not going to drag anyone else into it. Like I said before, I think everyone had done everything they could already.*

*It was looking like Gomer and John were going to get away with everything until this happened. They were vey successful at convincing a lot of people that I was the only one with the problem. Lori had a lot of sympathy from a lot of people. Most of them, outside of her family, were new friends of Gomer's. A lot of the people that have known us for a long time knew better than to believe everything Gomer was saying. On the other hand, I don't think people that knew us well really believed it had gotten as far out of hand as I was saying it was. I guess maybe I could not be very convincing because I couldn't believe it myself. I just didn't have a "smoking gun" or pictures to prove my suspicions. Now it may also come out about other women he has done this with. Not that I want that but if it has happened maybe they can get past this by coming out with it and start the healing process.*

*Thank you again. Say "Hi" to [your daughter] for me. I often wonder how you would explain this mess to her.*

*I hope your eyes are not bugging out from my small writing. Usually I write HUGE but all I have are two golf*

*pencils. If I write big they are dull right away and I can only sharpen them once a day.*
  *That's all for now. Love ya!*
  *Ken*


*Mom's Journal*
*No Date*
*"Promise you won't smash the cake into my face?"*
*"I promise if you promise."*
*"Promise."*
*It was that day that promises were made and by God, would be kept until death do us part. On that day we fed our wedding cake to each other as when my groom was permitted to kiss his bride for all to see as softly and gently as a butterfly landing on a rose; like a baby bird's beak opening wide trusting their mother to feed them, we fed one another sweet morsels of our wedding cake. And it was good.*
  *Today, twenty years and six days later, I wonder how, I wonder why, I wonder…. Though I still trust. However, my trust is fully in God and God alone. For the trust in my groom on our wedding day eroded to the protection order I have had to obtain to keep myself alive.*
  *Now promises broken, trust gone, but I still stand, papers eventually to be signed.*
  *Though I now stand.*


*Mom's Journal*
*March 16, 2007*
*What does a man profit from vindictive behavior?*
  *Do all forms of reason get thrown out the window, except for the one he holds like a greedy man with a sneering face and crouched body hoarding something to his breast that for the sake of his own insane pleasure will for*

greed and some plot that he withholds but spreads throughout the country.

I'm sure I'm really not making all that much sense, but I see him with that "I'll bet you wish you knew" look or that villainous cheshire grin you touted when I had to go. It takes great will power to keep your eyes, your teeth, your demon-like demeanor from chilling me to the bones. There is something so evil about you. How can you not see that your own flesh is rotting ever so slowly- gruesome indeed to think about. But it seems that everything about you that has made you a remotely decent person has gone to some dark and deceiving place. Some people can smell your rotting flesh and can see what a grotesque being you are letting yourself turn into. What evil has taken over you so fully? How much of that evil have you so falsely injected into the victims who blindly call you "hero" or "friend"? They are fools, nearly as much as you. Their boxes are so small; their minds so weak as though without defense or depth. Like little hobbits dancing around you, subjected to your outer charms. They are stupid. You are evil. Your blood must run as black as night, for it courses every part of you. You are not a man, and you don't even know it. You are so wrapped up in your decomposing skin. You fein the light of those who can't help but hold their noses when you are in their presence, their eyes watering. "Do you have a cold?" You sweetly ask as your forked tongue licks your thin and wicked lips.

Where is a full body mirror when you need one? You've obviously been avoiding mirrors, except to grab a quick glance that shows your cat smile is still there and readily available- no more- anything more than a glance would reveal truth. And part of your soul knows it.

It's that part that was taken from you many years ago. You mourn it deep down inside some cavern of your *innermost being- so far down, so pathetic in its crying innocence. Like a tear rolling down the cheek of someone whose spirit feels wounded. Like something that knows it will forever be forgotten less a brave and weary soul sets out on a treacherous journey to find it and bring it home, to let it once again see the light of day and smell the freshness in the spring air, and take joy in the presence of the plump robin singing lightly on the still dead lawn. It is like Christmas, opening a gift that is far more meaningful and of far greater value than anything anyone could ever give you. It's a gift to you from you. It gives you such awe and amazement that touches your soul, your spirit. You wonder at the warmth of the experience. Your body begins to feel slightly allow as you look at the back of your hand, the skin taking on a pinkish pale glow. No longer gray and decaying. "Oh my!" you gasp as you feel a stabbing pain in your heart that- like a lightning bold- pierces you deep inside. Your eyes widen with recognition. Something is happening to you- a metamorphosis you gander- yet- what's happening to me? You see your tattered old clothes transform into an outfit so clean and fresh and crisp, like laundry just taken inside from the clothes line in the summer the kind you just can't help burying your face in and breathing in thru your nose as deeply as you can. It's God's air. Ohhhh, how nice. Winter went awfully long this year didn't it? Upon looking up from your garments you see all of us looking at you, sort of with a look of wonder and placid concern. You're feeling it. "Is that it?" You curiously wonder, still experiencing a type of transitional bliss. A butterfly floating by gets your attention. In looking upward your eyes once again see the near expressionless gathering standing just a few feet away from you… As you gaze from face to face, slowly recognizing each one at some level, you feel a little prickly, because these people who you sense a vague connection to are merely staring straight back at your- expressionless, but not blank, you feel something melting, softening, sort of like when the Grinch begins to feel the meaning of Christmas. He begins to glow as his heart grows in size, nearly bursting that X-ray. Something like that. They keep watching, like waiting for someone to say something really important. Did I just hear a pin drop? I think so. Without even realizing what it is, goodness begins to flow, changing black to red, evil to good, hate to... oh my.*

*You feel it coming. You sort of squint at the slight sting. You touch your finder to the inner corner of your eye and feel moistness. You look at the liquid on the tip of your finger, then slowly stick out your tongue to sense the saltiness of the drop. A tear.*

*With a slight look of wonder, of uncertainty, your gaze once again meets the faces around you. It's hard to focus without blinking away the moisture. But if your eyes aren't deceiving you... Are they...? You look from face to face as you see them squinting and lifting their fingers to their eyes.*

*Something pricks your conscience. You feel confused, almost like a child feeling the guilt of a prank gone awry. You search your window thought, trying to remember a bit more than what he ate for supper last night. It's kinda laggy. He won't stop scanning his memory unit he remembers what he's trying to remember. Did you forget something?*

*Something in your middle twinges and your nose itches and begins to feel kinda large. You continue to scan through the mud of your memory. "What?!" You yell at yourself inside. "What is it? Where is it? What am I looking for that I can't find?!" He feels pressure. He looks at the people, some with trickles of salt water staining their faces.*

*Their eyes seem to ask "Will he find it?" There's a speck of anticipation and slight impatience in the air.*

*Will he endure the confusion of this earth that is almost rendering him desperate?*

*Will he lose patience with himself and yell at the top of his lungs, "Fuck- I can't do it! I can't find it!" And raise his arms desperately skyward as if talking to someone way up there some where. A slight but profoundly deafening silence follows, and his arms are slowly lowered in defeat, his heart heavy with loss. As he begins to walk away he turns his head to look back at all the people, their eyes cast downward in sorrow, turning mournfully away to go back from whence they came. Your back facing them, I see you shuffle toward the setting sun, dust kicking up in small clouds around your feet at each dragging step. I have to put my hand above my eyes to shade them from the bright light of the growing, then gradually shrinking, ball of wonder. As I squint to see you walk slowly away, the dust gradually builds up behind you, creating an opaqueness that barely reveals your graying shadow, oil no matter how hard I stare you are no more. I close my eyes. They sort of sting, but the warm glow of the magnificent light on the horizon helps form a smile of sweet content, a calm knowing that tomorrow the sun will return. And until my days on earth are done, there will always be a new tomorrow. I sigh, filling my lungs deeply with the smoothly delightful air of spring, turn, and with a little song in my heart and a little bounce in my step, I leave that place and go to my home where there is music playing, people laughing, connections deepening in the common joy and confidence they all share. I see Mom and Dad picking up their stride with arms outstretched, with tears of happiness, embracing, welcoming, tight. "We are so very proud of you honey" the sides of their faces pressed against mine. "We knew you could do it. We prayed so hard." "So did we," say the warm voices of the people walking toward me, arms outstretched. "We have been praying for you," says one; "And your family" said another. "I prayed that you would stay strong" said a person I recognized as my parent's neighbor. Then like a song each person revealing themselves, introducing me to people that I didn't know embracing those who knew. They had seen it somehow, understood the cruelty and the courage, the dementedness and the depth. I could see it on their faces as I was comforted and energized by each and every one; all those who believed even when they doubted. Then the crowd seemed to part off to the sides as though making room for someone royal to pass through. There I saw the sad but grateful faces of my two most beloved blessings. Our eyes meet and then as a musician building in energy and intensity, we moved toward one another laughing, crying, relating the tension, the anger, the frustration and confusion, embracing, purging the yucky through the salty secretion from eyes and nose.*

*There weren't enough Kleenexes, so we just let it flow over each other's shoulders; it didn't matter. This bond between mother and children, though bruised, was secure enough to last a lifetime. It was time to rest our aching hearts and breathe deeply of the air, so fresh, so fragrant, so new so... heavenly.*

My parents had the family divorce meeting in the fall of 2006 and my dad killed her on January 10, 2008. When I arrived home, I did what every good little freshman in high school does: finish his homework. The house was empty, which was incredibly common at the time so at first I thought nothing of it. After a short while, felicidal curiosity clawed at me so I looked around the house, noticing my mom's glasses were on the table, which was very odd because she needed those. But I ignored the red flag attempting to plant itself on my brainscape. The sweatpants and sweatshirt she was wearing when I left for school were strewn on her bed, with her cell phone sitting nearby. Another red flag ignored. *She's probably out jogging. Ya, that's why she doesn't have her glasses or phone. Nothing's wrong, let's go with that.* I succeeded in convincing myself despite the lack of anything like this happening in the past; she never left without her phone and she needed her glasses to see things. After a while I further explored the house and stopped at the top of the basement stares to see the laundry room light was left on. And so the ignored red flags trifecta was formed. We are Dutch- lights are not left on lightly, that was expensive fifty years ago. But never mind all that, I had a paper on Siberian Tigers to finish.

  Despite the willful ignorance, something was wrong and I knew it. I don't know how to describe it, whether it be "vibes" or intuition, but I knew something was wrong, really wrong. I returned to the top of the stares and stared down at the open door for a minute before descending. A dark vision flashed it's way into my mind: An image of my mom's body hunched over the laundry machine with her head submerged in the water filled tank. I can't explain why this happened. Was it a premonition? Was it dread? Or was I just sick in the head?

  I also remember waking up in the middle of the night before, thinking I heard something clattering around in the garage but my heavy head and sleepy eyes withdrew me back to slumber. Later, during the trial, I learned that my father had crawled into the attic late at night to wait for his moment.

  The last step arrived and I turned the corner. Lo and

behold there was her body in her red, stained, painting clothes with a nylon strap wrapped around her neck and tied to the rafter of the ceiling. Her face was turned away and I didn't see it until the funeral. A suicide, or so we all thought.

The adrenaline rush is nearly indescribable but I'll try anyway. It felt like every cell in my body was being stretched and torn apart like an old crusty rubber band- every muscle tight like a Siberian Tiger, and my entire brain an open wound. Any sense of self had disintegrated and there was nothing but there and now. It's hard to look back at those moments without a sense of awe and curiosity at the idea of achieving it again like some sort of psychological sadomasochism. You become so focused on the task at hand- dialing three numbers and communicating what lays before your eyes- nothing else matters. Something had to be done, even though I knew she was gone and hope was lost. I saw her lying there and helplessly shrieked, "MOM?!" without any expectation of a response. The Holland Sentinel said I was "shocked to peer over the railing of the basement stairs to see her lying in the laundry room." WRONG. The railing faced the opposite way of the laundry room which was at the bottom of the stairs to the left behind a wall and a door, you can't see inside the laundry room from the stairs. Why do you tell such lies?

With adrenaline cascading through my veins, my senses were gathered and I immediately ran up the stairs. The phone was already in my hand, I can't recall why. I don't remember what I said to the nice dispatch lady other than my mom was immobile on the floor and I hadn't touched her. She was incredibly kind and calm and guided me through those wretched moments very gently. Apparently this was recorded and used in the trial later. It makes me shiver to think of an entire crowd listening to that barely lucid conversation. She told me a police officer would arrive shortly so I waited and rampantly paced the house like a juggernaut, trying to forget about the wake of destruction I wanted to leave behind.

The first officer arrived at the house after a few long minutes. Since my dad was a cop, I knew most of the men and women on the force and he was a familiar face. He rushed down the stares, assessed the situation, and called in for support and an ambulance. Sgt. Belthouse was incredibly calm and kind throughout the whole process, of which I am eternally grateful.

Everything was going through my mind. One of them being, *Well at least I won't have to take exams now; but I also just wrote that paper for nothing.* My mom's dead, but I didn't have to do some busy work, so at least I had that going for me. Maybe fifteen minutes into this whole ordeal my dad came driving up to the house in his white Ford Escort. The first thing I noticed about him was a big chunk missing from his lower lip. He was wearing a hood, but the second I mentioned the lip, he took the hood off. My night of red flags was not over. I asked him how he received such a wound because I was skeptical and curious and he responded with a weak story about a Dutch Oven lid falling on his face during an attempt to retrieve it from the top of the kitchen cupboard. Ignorance is bliss so I might as well ignore that red flag too. Seemed legitimate and I didn't want to add the possibility of murder to my mind yet so I let it go. Plus he was a bit clumsy sometimes.

The officers and detectives who arrived at the scene began asking me all sorts of questions. Things like, "Did you move her or touch her? How long were you home? Were you at school all day?" There I sat absently answering the interrogation. My dad was out and about talking to the detectives- answering and asking questions. Eventually they sent me to the church across the street while they tried to reach my sister who was attending a school event. There we sat and waited while church people filtered into the building. The pastor attempted consoling and praying but none of it worked and I don't remember any of it. I was given a glass of water. It sat on the pastor's immaculate oak desk untouched in front of me. All I wanted in the world was to tip over that glass of water on his nice desk. It was my entire focus. I wanted to wreck something, but I refrained.

Looking back at it now, it feels like those red flags are so obvious. Although it doesn't matter because noticing them wouldn't have changed anything. I didn't know the specifics, but I did know something wasn't right. Your brain is their to protect itself and it can convince you of many things. At first those close to my dad believed him, as did I, when he told us the fallacy of the sutured lip. According to one of his closest friends, a mortician, he saw the lip and immediately grabbed him by the ears, examined him closely and deliberately, and asked if he had anything to do with it. He denied any involvement and we all wanted to believe him so the friend did too.

For a day after the death, no one knew it was murder or at least admit that's what they were thinking. While the mortician was examining the body he actually said aloud, "Boy, he really beat the shit out of her." This was before he had confessed and before the police even said they had their suspicions. The mortician went back a couple days later and asked his assistant if he had actually said that aloud, which was affirmed. We talked about it together and both agreed we believed the Dutch Oven Fallacy because we wanted to, not because we thought it was right. That bastard lied to the both of us- to everyone: his son, his family, and his best friends.

*From Dad,*
*Well actually the examiner was mistaken about "He beat the shit out of her." I didn't do any beating at all. If I was killing her purely out of anger maybe that might have been the case but I wasn't angry anymore, more like ambivalent towards her but not to what she was doing. I forget that, like most people, you may not know that for a time after a body dies it can still get bruised up and the medical examiner cannot tell if the bruises happened before or after death. I forget if I learned that in training or somewhere else like on a case. "Desperation" is a word I think would more accurately depict how I felt. Any marks on her that were seen by the examiner or anyone else came after she was dead and I was trying to get her suspended from the bathroom door first and the from the floor joists in the basement. Mom calling in sick that day threw a monkey wrench into what I had planned for after you and Bre went to school. I figured if she didn't show up for work that day that someone from church would have walked across the street to check on her. But alas, she called in sick and nobody else came to the house until you came home. If you ever want, I will tell you more details about all the things the investigators got wrong and all the misinformation given in court. The prosecutor showing the marks on her and saying I had "beat the shit out of her", played into their portrayal of me as being an abusive husband and father like Lori said I was. By the time of the trial, it didn't really make any difference anyway. I felt defeated and hopeless long before that so I didn't see any point in trying to refute anything they said.*

I am on the fence about this one. On one hand I get it, why even try. On the other, where is the pursuit and fight for the truth. Why ever give up on that? Maybe it was not his battle to fight. Maybe it is mine.

That night, after lingering at the church, we were sent to my aunt and uncle's house. I have no idea at what point my sister entered the picture. She was at an exam study thing at school when some officers went to collect her so either she came to the church or met me at my aunt and uncle's house. She once told me she wished herself to be the one that found her but I disagree.

About twenty-four hours after arriving at my new home, there was another blow: my father confessed to murder. Keith and Jan were the ones with him before he went to the confession room. Ten years after the murder, at The Windmill eating breakfast, was was when they told what happened. They were all waiting at the station, when an officer called Ken into a private room. He looked at Keith and Jan and said, "I did this to Lori. Now do what you do best and take care of my children." The fumbled around not knowing exactly what this meant. Surely he meant "I did this" in some metaphorical way by driving her crazy enough to kill herself. Lo and behold, the office came out and told them Ken had confessed to murder. Jan collapsed as Keith started angrily yelling all these questions, unlike him, but apparently the officer thought they had already known. Why did so many people think anyone could have seen this coming? "What am I supposed to tell the kids?!"

Apparently Ken had crawled up into the attic while we were all sleeping and waited silently until my sister and I left for school. My mom wasn't actually supposed to be there either. It was one of those days where she worked, which weren't many, but she had called in sick and as he said, this threw a monkey wrench in his plan. He intention was for someone besides his child to find the body. In the confession my dad said he knew this was his chance after seeing her in the doorway. The bloody lip was because my mom bit off some flesh amidst the struggle. Both of them struggled, but he managed to get a better grip and strangle her to death. In the throws of death, Lori managed to wheeze out, "Think of the children." To which he replied, "I am" and "continued to tighten his grip" as the testimony states.

Since my dad was a cop and had done some research, he tried to cover it up and make it look like a suicide. He failed. He bought the nylon strap and the gloves but left the receipts in his car, which were quickly discovered by the detectives. I wouldn't doubt he subconsciously knew he couldn't get away with it. With all this back story there is an evident motive, the first thing the detectives attempt to decipher. At least according to *Law and Order: SVU*.

Between the murder and confession we barely spoke except for the small amount at our house the night before. Twenty-four hours later, while everyone was hanging around the house, my uncle Keith walked through the front door with a solemn and empty look on his face. He said one sentence: "Ken confessed to murder and will be put away for a long time." Instant eruption of tears and wails. I was cradled in the arms of a good family friend and remember weeping and trying to pick out the details of the Hebrew ring he was wearing on his thumb, in hopes of distracting myself from the god-awful reality into which I was thrown. It didn't work; nothing ever does.

So began my life at Keith and Jan's. For a few nights my sister and I shared a bed because being alone was just too much and were hardly left by ourselves in general. The difference between being asleep and awake was difficult to distinguish for quite some time. Looking back, I'm not sure if being in a crowd was right because I have always liked to process things in solitude and silence. While I have no regrets, solitude is where I have learned the most about myself, including how to respond to this situation. When you spend time in purposeful solitude, you realize much of your perceived personality is merely a response to social cues. Being alone allows you to focus on yourself and allows you to figure out how to meaningfully project your will to the world. In the end, you can make either way work and it's really about letting time pass. Time really does heal all wounds. When a bone is fractured, when a plant stem snapped, it grows back stronger than before.

*Dad's Letter*
*Friday June 20, 2008*
*Dear Keith,*

*Oh brother, I so wish I could talk with you. So many things I think about I would love to share with you. For the last few days I've been thinking, "I wonder what God has in mind with all this?" over and over again. You and I both know it will work out for the best somehow and some way but it's awfully difficult to see how at this point.*

*I think about how you and Jan are fairing often. I know you are doing well but I just wonder how it's going. Each of the kids has their quirks about them. Toph is very analytical like Lori's dad and he doesn't like change too quickly. Paul's parents never told him when they were going on vacation until the morning they were leaving because if they told him earlier he would worry the whole time and would not sleep for days before. On the other hand that enabled him to be a research scientist. I think Toph is well on his way to using his giftedness too. So is Bre but just in a different way. Both Bre and Toph are a lot of fun so I hope you are using that and enjoy that.*

*You wrote in your last letter that I'm still your "Kenny man." You have no idea what that means to me. I could never have asked for a better big brother. I know that this must be really pushing you to the limits so I appreciate it even more. So often a lot of the things I did, I did because I wanted you to be proud of me and you always were. Not that I did them just for you but in the back of my mind I would always look forward to telling you. On the other hand you were always my go to person when I had a problem. I can remember you and Jan being there for me and lot of other people way back in 1976. 76! Wow you guys must be old. That's what makes this so hard. I know I've disappointed you and Jan and then, even though your great hearts are willing to take it on, I dumped a huge challenge in your lap. So, like I said, "What does God have in mind with all this?"*

*For myself, I look back to the example of you and Jan from back in 1988 and onward. I realize that I have no idea how hard it was to move off the farm to your house in Zeeland but you both made the best of it and God blessed that. I think you would agree that everything has worked out for the best. Right away you had so much more time to spend with Jan and the girls. That alone was priceless and you certainly made the best of it with your family and so many other kids. I was always proud of you guys too. A little envious at times but you always shared in your hospitality.*

*That makes me want to make the best of it in my little world as it is now too. Jay is the guy next to me that was really flipping out and angry at everyone when they first moved him next to me. He saw me reading the Bible and since he can't read, I read some stories to him. Now he asks me everyday to read Bible stories to him. He has calmed down a lot and hasn't cussed anyone out for two days. That's my little world but I hope I can make a difference. Often I think, "What would Jesus do?" so often in the past.*

*I'll get this letter and the letter to Topher out to you.*

*Mom's Journal
October 21, 2007
I have so many thoughts swirling in my head. I feel restless and somehow alone. I miss Barb. I miss laughing with her. I miss her friendship. I miss her way of saying it like it is. I feel so warn down from Ken's wrath and power. I want peace. I want security. I want to be loved without expectation or condition or some standard that needs to be met by someone who considers themselves sent by God to condemn and correct. What would Jesus say? What would Jesus do? Would he take sides? It just seems to me that God uses some very unconventional ways to get his people to notice him in very deep and profound ways, I sure would like it if Jesus were out on his Sunday afternoon stroll right now, and why his robes flowing in the warm autumn wind would already know that I am sitting out on my swing pondering, wondering, seemingly alone in my thoughts about life. I know he would definitely put me at ease, because he's just that kind of person. I would see it in his eyes- that he cares, that he understands. I wonder if I would be selfless enough to offer him a cup of cool water. I would like to think so- he's done that so many times for me. Literally. I think we would sit here for a little bit, simply enjoying the warm and sunny day. He'd pet Tipper as she would go to him and rub up against him with affection. I think we would exchange pleasantries about the weather. I would thank him for it. He'd smile at me as though I had made a goofy funny, though he knows how much I truly appreciate this warmth and light during the days that grow dismally shorter and darker and colder. He already knows how that can wear me down.*

*So where would we begin? Would he tell an early story with a heavenly meaning? Would my ears understand it? Would he just start telling the story of my life even though I've already lived it thus far? Would I hear something I never heard before? Something that would send me into a sort of self loathing or perhaps tears would well up in my eyes, because he feels my pain and confusion that have plagued me more than once? I would desire to be like the Syrophoenician woman who responds to Jesus' words with, "Maybe dogs eat the crumbs under the table, but surely if God cares enough about dogs to feed them, wouldn't he consider me too- unworthy as I am but full of respect that permeates from the soul." I need to feel that somehow God sees to my very depths of how much I want to serve him, of how much I want to live my life as an offering. Because I do. Will Jesus call me a hypocrite (since that word keeps surfacing lately) or would he acknowledge the hypocrites around me? Either way, I'd probably end up crying just for the sheer possibility that the One who has all the answers sitting right near me on my front deck (Tipper is now curled up in his lap as Jesus gently strokes her).*

*It seems that nearly every time I turn to the scriptures I am reminded of God's love, his passion for his people, his strength and knowledge beyond all understanding; that he is in control, worthy of our trust and to be trusted. He is patient, slow to anger, but if we need to be corrected, he'll do it. It has been said time and again that if some one screws with us, it is his job to punish, not mine. Over and over again I read that I am responsible for my own conduct, my own faith efforts; I am not responsible to seek vengeance or power or control in ways that God takes no pride in. Evil results when we take matters into our own hands. It all seems so very clear to me. It is so black and white nearly every time I open my Bible.*

*God love me and he will take care of me. In so many ways he has done this thought my life- that's why I am the way I am now. Perseverance, humility, patience, mercy, kindest, meekness produce rewards of deep joy and containment, or strength and courage- unknown to common man. I truly believe that God reveals himself in a way that is as unique as each and everyone of us is. He connects us where we're at. BUT in the same breath we must choose to want it, look for it, and even long for it. And how sweet when his love is revealed to us.*

*I'll admit that I am just as human as Adam and Eve, but inclusive, I want to feel the loving embrace of God's perfect arms. This is where I find my comfort. He knows my every struggle and my depths tell me that he admires and honors what my soul desires. Learning unconditional love has not exactly been conventional, but truly and undoubtedly God breathed. All you have to do is look at how Jesus lived to make God's point. Jesus shows people that who, what, and how we love God is not to be stifled or judged by manmade rules and policies that fit societal standards. God commands us to love one another- whatever it takes. Love is patient and kind- not rude, vindictive and abrasive. It is tender and understanding - not forceful and self-centered. Love is selfless and giving- even to death. Love is defined by God's laws, not man's. The struggle for me seems to rest or wobble somewhere in between.*

*Are those unconventional acts of love which are so God-like really from God? I just don't see how they can't be from him. It just seems that people who don't understand this can only see things from Pharisee-like platforms, looking down, judging, concluding. I just don't believe that that is how God operates. Again, look at the life of Jesus and who he associated with. He has given me living water just like any other unclean person he has associated with.*

*How can people like the Pharisees NOT see this? As Patti would say, they must be Stoo-pid! Divorce, not taken to very well in the God-fearing community, for me has been God's way of lifting me up out of the miry clay- to be taken, formed, used for and by him as a message of freedom- not like hippie freedom to do whatever, but freedom to serve God openly, practicing wisdom and Jesus like acceptance. I KNOW that to be true already and I foresee a future largely linked to sharing God's word, his strength, his love- in ways that the folks with tunnel vision will refuse or can't see as truth.*

*Perhaps in part and for this reason I look at my past experiences of depression, of neglect and abuse, of self doubt, of a broken marriage- sucky, yes, but to be somehow acknowledge as good, for they have made me who I am today. They have, at times, made me go crawling into God's arms, into his love and strength because there was nowhere else to go. I have forgiven, I have gotten past much bitterness and anger, with joy and peace resulting. I do not understand someone's desire to bring forth everything supposedly wrong in my life for the whole world to see. Its mercy and meekness gone very sour, no doubt. Such need and obsession will only be fodder for eternal fire if you ask me. It is not, despite the ease of it, my job to judge others. It is my job to seek God. This job comes with eternal rewards, peace of mind and heart, and unshakeable depth of joy. This is how God moves in me. Thanks be to God.*

# Chapter 4: The Trial

*Dad's Letter*
*Sunday July 27, 2008*
*Dear Keith,*
    *It was so good to talk to you last weekend. To hear about how well the kids are doing and all the stories of people caring for each other and supporting each other was wonderful. I knew going through with the trial would be difficult for a lot of people but I envisioned a time of people coming out with issues and feelings that they probably would not have been able to otherwise. For that reason, I'm glad I went through with the trial. I hoped and prayed the good things that would happen would outweigh the bad and I trust that that did happen. I've heard from several people that there was a benefit of getting together for the trial so that is encouraging.*
    *[Someone] said that you, Bre and Toph went to [the storage unit] and went through some of the stuff there. I would imagine that was a little easier now after the trial is over. Of course I only know what you related to [sister] and she to me but it sounds like that was a healing experience also. I'm sure I can't even think of half of the stuff anymore since I was gone for two and a half of the last three and a half years but I'm sure there is a ton of stuff. I hope you have found my GPS, and all the stuff with it. I kind of miss "my stuff" but I'm happy to see it go to good use.*
    *[She] is sending pictures of the kids from during your cooking class. She said even in the picture you can see they are having a good time.*
    *I'm glad you are telling me honestly about how the kids are reacting to me. Even what Toph said about the shirt he was wearing to the trial. So far anything you've*

told me isn't near as bad as what I was telling myself in my head.

I got a very nice letter from [a friend]. She thinks the world of our family and may be getting in touch with you. [She] wants to connect at some point so they need to get each other's numbers. [She] told me about the interactions between you [and others] and wants to thank each for your support and love at the trial. She even said she wouldn't trade any of it and doesn't regret anything even after having to go to the trial.

Several people ask if Bre and Toph are going to therapy yet. I tell them that as far as I know they have not but that they do have a lot of other love and support. I included the article about the VA using a new slogan to get Vets to use the suicide hotline. The line "It takes the courage and strength of a warrior to ask for help" caught my attention. That line of thought may be helpful for Toph since he more than likely gets his stoic demeanor from me and that slogan struck a chord with me.

I love you brother. You and your family are the greatest and I know Bre and Toph are in the greatest of care possible. You say you worry about me but my biggest of worries is for Bre and Toph. However, those worries are wonderfully assuaged by knowing where they are and it makes everything much easier to take. I think about Jan never having a brother or a son really until now, at least not living with one, and wonder how that goes. I'm sure it's a little different but if he's gaining weight I'm sure he doesn't complain. He and Bre were always such a blessing together.

One thing that bums me out is [Guy and Girl Oldfriends]. I remember their first date so well, their wedding, and I even know what there first argument was about- [Girl] wanting to take all kinds of pictures of all the *waterfalls they saw while on a trip out west. [Guy] could have pictures of two Christmases on one roll of film and think he had all the pictures of a year that he needed. No kidding! I think he did that during college. Well it just really makes me sad. Especially after getting to know their son in Lacrosse last year. I felt bad about their name and situation coming out in the trial but since they are getting a divorce anyway I guess it didn't matter that much. Did [Guy] say anything about that? I've thought about writing him, did he say anything about that?*

*[She] asked me about what will happen at sentencing. I don't know much about what will happen there although if [Lori's parents] are allowed to say something I'm sure they will. Be ready for that as much as one can be.*

*Keith, I will say that I don't worry about you and I don't worry about how either of you are doing but please know that I think of each of you often in thankfulness and in prayerful concern.      I love you all.*

*Love Ken*


*Mom's Journal*
*April 15, 2007*
*How does he possibly think he can get away with some of this stuff? An email stating he had picked up some cooking stuff this past weak- who the hell does he think he is? Is he above the law that he can violate a PPO whenever he damn well pleases? He gets what he wants, bar non. It just never ends. That email put me in such a "Who do you think you are?!" mode- enough to go into the bedroom and purge the room of all of his shit and dump it on the bed of the downstairs bedroom. I piled it all up in a heap on the bed where shattered glass may still be. I hope so. Dare I find pleasure in him putting something on, a tiny*

*piece of glass lodging somewhere- stinging pain and plenty of blood. Barely a token in exchange for how he treated me with his nasty ways. At this point I think that jail time sounds graciously inadequate and painless compared to what he has so purposefully put me through. I just want to scream at him to leave me alone! Stop being an asshole for God's sake. Use the fucking mail service instead of the kids and every other method you're not supposed to use. What are you trying to prove? Are you greater than God that you think your putrid actions go unnoticed? How do you trust God to fit your self-centered world? Surely he sees your evil, even when others prefer blindness and fein ignorance to reality. They are fools as much as you. Every passage God leads me to (which are plenty!) reminds me of the outcome, the consequences, of your cruelty and desire to control YOUR world. Eventually, God will reveal himself fully to you, but it will be too late. You will be crushed- like the serpent's head. His head will dig deeply into your undeserving soul. You will beg for mercy but God and everyone else will shake their head at the foolish stupidity of your actions. Too bad, too late! It's time to pay the piper- you lose. You lose you lose you lose.*

*I have always been a winner in God's eyes' I just didn't always feel it amid the fortune of life. God knows my heart better than I do. He knows my thoughts and he reveals his. He is my final judge for my life- no human could be so fair as he. Period. He speaks to my heart the way nobody else will or can. Bar none. I know I know I know!*

*Mom's Journal*
*May 16, 2007*
*Today from a distance I saw you walking away and I was glad because I hate it when you walk toward me. The hair on the back of my neck begins to prickle. My stomach*

*lurches and the rate of my heart increases as anxiety quickly sets in. I try not to show the panic that races inside me.*

*I have papers inside a ziplock bag inside my zipped up purse that say you can walk but you'd better keep my distance. If I was able to have a bright orange line encircling me at a 500 ft radius with signs that say "Do not cross. Violators will be prosecuted." You'd invariably put at least a toe on that line. More likely, you'd have one foot in and one foot out like you're doing the Hokey Pokey, playing some kind of game with my mind. You already know you're good at that. Like shortly after you trusted too hard and these very papers you've served to others came into your own hands, your evil ego walked right up to me at a school performance. My body shook the whole drive home even while talking to the kids. Why didn't I unzip my phone from my purse and call 911? I should have.*

*I have gotten wiser since then; so now when I see you walking my way, no matter what the distance, my hand just naturally goes to my connection to your work! Keep your distance.*

*Letter from J+K to Ken,*
*Dear Ken,*
*I have held off writing until now as I have felt there wasn't anything I could say that was of any value. When you lived here with us, I always spoke open and honestly with you as did Keith. We'd give our opinions and share our thoughts clearly stating how our views came from "The back row of the bleacher seats" and how we had no first hand knowledge or experience. Now however, we are front row and center of attention.*

*Keith and I have given this much thought and prayers and in that we simply share our hearts.*

*Ken, we understand what you want for John Doe, your feeling toward his "care" for your wife and the destruction of your family. You appropriately sent charges to the state level to expose and punish him. You have brought his name and reputation to the forefront in this community and exposed his unprofessional care. For these reasons Ken, John will suffer the rest of his life, so to that end you have achieved in your goal. The balance and continued damage for John will come from his past patients. Ken, you have succeeded in your quest to damage and destroy John. You said you did what you have done for the love you had for your children, so in that love we continue this letter. In truly loving your children as we do, we ask you to prayerfully consider what we have to say.*

*A trial stands ahead of us- the raw, horrible pain, hurt and trauma revisited. The three people you love most in life- Bre, Toph, and Keith will endure such heartache you have no idea, not to mention the rest of your immediate family and the ripple effect to all DeKleines as well as the collateral damage so many others will suffer.*

*Ken, you have now given your children the life you had so desired they have so we are asking you to do one last thing for them. The only decent thing left you can do as well as the last gift you can give to bre and Christopher. Please plead this case out and stop it from going to trial. Don't let these children suffer anymore. Give them the freedom to continue moving forward in life and plead guilty.*

*Ken, when you walked away from us at Zeeland Police Department back in January, you looked us right in the eyes and asked us to "take care of" your children. Now Ken, we're begging you to trust us in our care for them and all that is best for them. Please, take care of these babies one last time and plead guilty.*

*Please know this is not a letter we write easily. We pray for you as you consider this and the gift you can give to Bre and Christopher.*

During the week of the trial, a family friend lent us their beach house in Grand Haven, Michigan, closer to the Court House. So believe it or not, that week contains more positive memories of beach sand and golf swings than anything having to do with the trial. It took me way too long to realize this was on purpose. Not many were letters written about the trial because it was not a fun time for anyone involved.

The local news covered most of it, but they also got a lot of details wrong, mostly about the actual murder. Mainly details about that night and how it all happened. Of course they built up the whole victim issue, highlighting domestic violence. At first, this upset me, but it's still a good thing to bring into the conscious of the public and if my father needs to be that scapegoat, I'll volunteer him as tribute. He's not going anywhere and his public image is already as low as possible so what more could hurt? Thanks to modern technology and the internet, many of these journalistic masterpieces are on YouTube. It allows the public to be well informed and leave wise commentary like the savant Icepick00000 so eloquently comments, "That nigga tuck me to jail one time lol hell naw." Maybe he should be the one writing this book.

Fortunately I only had to testify one day, had my outfit planned and everything. I was going to wear my favorite T-Shirt from Wes Anderson's *The Life Aquatic*- the one with the Zissou Insignia- and my word was final. Jan asked me to wear something nicer, to which I said, "No" and nothing was pushed beyond that, bless her heart. Before going into the court room, I debated for a solid half hour on whether or not I needed to take a poo. I went to the bathroom, but it was a false alarm and figured it was just nerves but it was nice to get away from everyone for a second before it all went down.

    The trial was everything that is bullshit. I hated it- all of it. No one, not even my father thought I should be involved but the prosecutor deemed it was necessary to paint a portrait for the Jury of my father's guilt and my dad needed a trial to capsize the John Doe boat. I still am skeptical as to why I was there. He confessed, what more do you need? Why do I need to get involved? Horse shit. They used me and I felt used. My dad is still a bit to blame for that one because he could have called the trial off, but he had specific things he wanted to reveal and I'll take that hit if it reveals a predatory therapist.

    Since I am unable to recall actual experiences from the trial for myself, interviews and articles have been a key source of information, despite my distaste and distrust for the despotic media. According to MLive, a Michigan news site, the prosecutors produced evidence that made my mom not look like a monster and disputed evidence that made my mom look like an unfit mother. But all the evidence I've see points to the contrary.
Did they ever ask me, her child?
Does a fit mother make her son cook his own meals after school!?
Does a fit mother make her high school son launder his own clothes!?
Does a fit mother disappear without notice while I wretch in pain and call fifteen times!?
Does a fit mother avoid being in her own home!?
Does a fit mother fuck her therapist while her husband is serving his country!?

That's about enough of that. She was a terrible mom and that is the plain truth. Any other conclusion is delusion. During one lacrosse game in eighth grade, I happened to score a miraculous goal. My dad was there to see it and called my mom immediately after my masculine feat. He thought she was at an appointment with John. However, when he called, he found out she was at one of John's kid's soccer games instead because "Their mom wasn't able to go so they needed a mom to watch them." What a joke. I'm sure it had nothing to do with the fact that John was the head coach of the team.

The reality is that people, most often the mothers, are using claims of abuse to manipulate the system in order to win custody or asset in divorce court. As reported by the West Virginia Department of Health and Human Resources Child Protective Services (2007) 37,165 claims of abuse were made. Of which, only 3,998 were found to be valid. Of all those, 10% of abuse claims were valid.

According to Answers.com, "In the cases where fathers do challenge for custody, 60% of them will be accused of child sexual abuse as a tactic by the mother to prevent him getting it. If he does win custody, he can than be accused of domestic violence committed some time in the previous 12 months, at which point an injunction *stops him from getting the child until he can prove himself innocent*. If he does prove himself innocent, or it was found that *he defended himself when she attacked him*, then he cannot have custody because that's still considered domestic violence against the mother." Apparently a man can't defend himself according to modern Divorce Law. Apparently men are guilty until proven innocent according modern Divorce Law.

That poor bastard never saw these claims coming and made some dire mistakes because of it- e.g. climbing through the window, approaching her and breaking his PPO, breaking into her office- all things that were held heavily against him, legally and understandably. This was back in 2008 when we didn't yet know about the common place false accusations of this magnitudes. Now upon further research there are catalogues of websites full of legal advice for men who are falsely accused and despite the frequency of these lies the law still hasn't changed. False abuse accusations are a legal epidemic.

Upon mere claims of abuse, the mother is given full custody of the children. This separation gives the mother plenty of time alienate the children from the father through purposefully malicious coaching sessions and social subversion.

She once told me my dad was molested as a child on the farm and got into some gritty detail. When I asked him about whether or not this happened, he was shocked about "How far she went in her attempt to degrade me" because apparently she was telling multiple people, mainly her own family this molestation misinformation in order to inspire fear of him molesting my sister, which she had already threatened.

According to MLive, a Michigan Website,

"The Prosecutor, Ron Frantz, said DeKleine misportrayed his wife as a bad wife and mother who was mentally unstable.

In fact, Frantz said, 'Lori DeKleine was simply trying to get out of a bad marriage'. A judge in 2007 agreed she should get temporary custody of their two teen children and 'we also know Lori was a capable and dependable co-worker at her church.'

'There is indeed another side to it,' Frantz said, suggesting that Lori DeKleine had no serious mental issues.

Frantz said Ken DeKleine sought to control his estranged wife, even surreptitiously accessing her church computer two days before the death and accessing e-mail where she take with others about her divorce and prepared for a seminar on women in abusive relationships. Lori DeKleine's case was going to be a topic at the seminar. Frantz said DeKleine had plenty of motive for the killing and having it seen as a suicide.

'His public image stays intact, there is no stalking seminar revelation and he and [girlfriend] can now go public,' he said, referring to a woman DeKleine was dating

While DeKleine's attorney argued he killed Lori DeKleine for the sake of the children, Frantz said that was illogical.

'How in the world would it ever be under any circumstances in your children's best interest to murder their mother?' he asked."

According the Grand Rapids Press:
"Former Holland Police Officer Ken DeKleine, convicted Friday of killing his wife, Lori, partially blamed his broken family on her psychologist, who -- testimony showed -- had a sexual relationship with her.

But Ottawa County Prosecutor Ronald Frantz said the 'psychologist, [John Doe], was just a focus for DeKleine's anger toward his wife, whom he sought to control.'

'He knows better than to get involved with a client, that's true. I'm not going to defend that,' Frantz said of [Doe] on Friday while addressing the jury.

[Doe] is not charged with any crime.

[Doe's] state license was suspended in February for at least six months and one day. He can re-apply for it, but re-instatement is not automatic, according to reports obtained Friday from the state Department of Community Health.

The documents detail the relationship [Doe] developed with Lori DeKleine, who previously was diagnosed with bi-polar mood disorder

In private practice at Westshore Family Psychology in Holland, [Doe] provided psychotherapy to Lori DeKleine from April to November 2004.

The following summer, they began a personal relationship while he continued to treat her, reports said.

The state said [Doe] "failed to recognize that a personal relationship violated the therapist-client relationship ... (and) also failed to recognize his responsibility to prevent the development of inappropriate relationships between clients and family members."

The relationship continued through March 2007 and included Lori DeKleine visiting [Doe] and his wife, occasionally staying overnight.

[Doe] also accepted gifts from Lori DeKleine, including birthday presents for his children. She also looked after his children at times, reports said.

The report said [Doe] and/or his spouse would meet socially with both DeKleines.

[Doe], reached at home, declined to comment. State reports did not describe a sexual relationship, but a detective testified in Ken DeKleine's trial that [Doe], after an initial denial, later admitted a sexual relationship with Lori DeKleine."

Frantz you incompetent dingus. I hope you read this

book to find that you are shit at your job. Testimony showed Doe had sexual relationship with Lori, but you think John was just a focus for Ken's anger and control. A Dependable co-worker? Did you even ask her coworkers? They claimed to be walking on egg shells around Lori because she was so irrationally unpredictable. Suggesting Lori DeKleine had no serious mental illness!? Did you even look at her medical history and her confirmed diagnoses?

    My guy, looks like a lot of your prosecution was based off of lack of information. You are a disgrace to the legal system Ron Frantz. It is in my, the child's, best interest that my mother be dead if she is ACTUALLY INSANE. Illogical my ass you shallow thinking prick. If you know how to read and have read *To Kill a Mockingbird,* you would understand that even the great wise Atticus understands what needs to be done with a mad dog.

    Why did Frantz not have all this information that so easily negated his claims? Maybe my insults aren't justified and here's why. My dad put up zero fight in court. He had all this information but none of it was used, which is why Frantz didn't see it. I get it though, dad definitely killed her and is definitely going to jail, so why struggle when the noose is already taut? He gave up. He gave up because no one had been listening to him for years and no one was going to listen to him now. I've listened, I've learned and I thank God for my father's sacrifice every single day.

    The judicial system in regards to divorce is a disgrace. Even if the abuse claims are proven to be false, no one hears about it and the reputation of the accused is torn and shattered. There is no doubt in my mind that this tactic is being used on various levels, including political.

    The Prosecution played me off as a victim of Ken,

but felt more like a victim of them. Justice must prevail. It was practically useless information as well. All they did was ask me questions like "Is this your house?" and "What happened when you got home?" All the shit I had already told a detective in more detail than I gave the jury. They even lied to me and said I wasn't going to be in view of my father. I entered the room and immediately made eye contact with him. No expressions were made. And there I sat on the podium trying to avoid looking right at his ugly mug.

Even though my father knew I was going to have to be there and knew it would suck for me, he had an agenda that he had to stick with. He could have plead guilty and let the whole thing go instead of taking it to trial but his goal was to bring the John Doe situation into the spot light. The detectives and the prosecutors eventually caught on and his wishes were granted. John Doe ended up losing his license for six months and one day. If it was just six months, all he would have to do is reapply for his license, but the one day extra meant he had to go through the whole shebang of acquiring his license again, which means he would have to go back to school and re-earn his degree. Apparently he lived in Holland for a while and worked in Grand Rapids, although I don't know what he is doing, nor do I care.

I once ran into John a few months after the murder. This was before I knew anything about the nasty relationship he had with my mother so, to me, he was still a friendly face. I was all smiles and small talk and in retrospect, I can see his face of discomfort because he knew many things I didn't. Many years later, I saw him with his wife in downtown Holland. I was in my car thankfully, but my blood started to boil and I lost my train of thought in a red flash of rage. I kept driving with white knuckles while imagining hitting him in his fat fucking face.

Many other people had to testify as well: family, coworkers, friends- all had their time on the podium. "All I know is his wife is dead", said the Chief of Police, his boss. "It appeared to be maybe a suicide and I said 'We are not going to get involved in this investigation. We are to secure the scene and the Ottawa County is going to respond.' When Ottawa County got there, it didn't take long to find out and to look at it and say 'We got some real questions here'."

The detectives were very sympathetic with my father's demands. They told Keith how astounded they were with my father. They said he was incredibly cooperative and mentioned how even though he killed her, he still managed to have so much love for his children and even his estranged wife.

When I spoke to my father the first time, I asked him a lot about the day of the murder. He told me what I believe to be the truth but included a lot of distasteful comments about my mom, which he later apologized for. He highlighted the fact that she and him had many good times and positive memories as well. My parents, both of them, did many things well and I like to think my sister and I are evidence of it. That time I spoke to my dad, he made another point to make sure I knew all the positive ways mom influenced me as well. He's right. From her I got compassion, a love for the Beatles, a love for art, an accepting attitude, and an appreciation for the little things.

Despite the confession, I was confused on whether or not it was a premeditated murder. It wasn't until I got a few details that it was solidified. My father had a conversation with one of his friends about forensics- how to commit murder and the consequences. The guy told him anyone would be crazy to try and do anything like this because of how advanced forensics science had gotten. This conversation came up in the trial. He was hiding in the attic, waiting until the house was empty so he could go in and search the house for more adultery evidence. The fact that she wasn't supposed to be home was what made me think it wasn't premeditated like everyone was saying.

    I was wrong. He had the idea for a year and sat on it. Even went to McDonalds after he killed her. Quentin Tarantino should take some notes. Ken constantly sought advice from damn near everyone he knew, including his kids, which was exhausting for everyone to say the least. He wanted his kids to have a normal family, something that was hopeless for us unless he did something crazy and the dream of having that kind of life had long dwindled at this point. Maybe if he had thought it through more, he would have realized Bre only had one year of high school and I only had two. It wouldn't have been long until we were both out of the house and creating our own lives outside of the both of them. If he had sat on the evidence and waited instead of sperging out, maybe I would have been enlightened eventually. Welp, too late.

    Ken thought about murder for a year and eventually decided to bring it to fruition. He had been to a police seminar where he learned a nylon strap would be a great way to kill someone. A quick trip to the Storage and Organization aisle at Lowes was all he needed, although the dumb dumb managed to leave those receipts in his car, as well as leave remnants of his own blood in the house. Clearly he never saw *Dexter;* it's all about the tarps and cellophane- throw them up and take them down then throw it in the ocean; come on man, this is murder not rocket surgery. In the trial, he admits the second he walked in the house and saw her, he knew this was the time to make the move. He almost got away with it until the detective saw his foot print, but I think the blood and obvious motive would have given him away anyway, considering all the divorce proceedings and PPO. The fact he had thought about it for so long contributes to his lack of regret. He knew what he was doing. Over loquacious internet strangers often say things like, "That fucker thought he could get away with it." The fact that he quickly confessed has determined that is a lie.

Many of the people that loved him had to testify against him. I was about to say I can't imagine what that was like, but then I remembered been there done that; I know exactly what it's like. There are plenty of YouTube videos of the trial so most of the media "research" comes from those recordings. All I want to know now is who the hell clicks the "Thumbs Up" on these videos; greasy bastards. I tried to get a manuscript of the entire trial, but it would have cost me thousands of dollars even though I thought it would be under the Freedom of Information Act, a more apt named being The Freedom To Pay A Lot For This Information Act. The police chief was asked if he ever saw any warning signs, to which he replied, "My job was to make sure he could perform his job and he did his job. Now what he suppressed inside of him… I mean, you can suppress something inside of you and I can be your best friend and if you don't want me to know it, I'm not going to know it." Ken did not tell anyone about this and made sure absolutely no one knew.

My grandma testified, "Ken took upon the role of God and ended Lori's life here on Earth." Can't help but agree with you on that one, grandma; dick move on his part. They requested he be sent to general population (Gen Pop), probably hoping he'd get a good ruttin' or two, but the request wasn't granted and he was originally quarantined with other ex-cops. Now enough time has passed where people have forgotten the whole ordeal, so he is currently with the general population and he is safe there, despite what *Shawshank Redemption* will have you believe. Two people, friends from church, were there when he was charged with murder. They told the media, "He's a good man. He just did something really bad. But we know that's not the person we knew."

*Dad's Letter*
*Tuesday June 10, 2008*
*Dear Keith and Jan,*
    *Today seems like it should be the last day of school. Bre and Toph have been out for almost two weeks already. It just doesn't seem right.*
*Wednesday June 11, 2008*
    *I got your letters today. I'm sure they were very difficult letters to write but I'm glad you were upfront with me and let me know what you were thinking about the trial and about the phone calls and letters. For phone calls, is there any way I could call your cell phone? If that wouldn't work that will be OK but I thought if that could be an option it may be something better. I think [someone] was going to look into getting calls on his cell phone a while back but I don't know what he found out.*
    *As for the trial, I am waiting to hear from [Lawyer] about what the forensic report says before considering any options. I don't think the forensic test went very well because I know I wasn't able to communicate very coherently because of having to stop all the time as he wrote down everything I said word for word. It's not*

*something you can prepare for at all. As more time passes since January, I realize how tense I was, how easily angered I was, and how impulsive I was for the two years I had been home from Iraq. When I came home I was not prepared for what I came home to and went from the frying pan into the fire. Either way it was hell on the kids and either way, I'll keep the best interest of everyone in mind when I talk to Farmer. I know I've always tried to do that. Sometimes I did very well, sometimes I did very poorly. It's easy now to think about all the times I screwed up but I know I did well most of the time. I think Bre and Toph were turning out pretty incredible. Not perfect but still pretty amazing in a lot of ways.*

*I would often think of you Keith when I was trying to decide what was best for Lori, Bre, and Toph. However, sometimes it was frustrating because sometimes there are problems that nobody knows how to handle and there is not going to be a good outcome no matter what.*

*I never told anybody a story from many years ago but now seems like a good time to for some reason. It's from back in 1985-86 when Scooter was two to three years old. You guys were living in the farm house and I had taken a year off from college. Scooter was at that really fun imaginative play age and I just loved that about her. I was spending a lot of time at your house helping on the farm and stuff so I played a lot with Scooter and Boop. Especially when you, Keith, were gone for some reason. One time when you were gone I had lunch in the house and played a little while with Scooter. She was the nurse and I was the patient who had a "fever." I got countless shots, had my heart checked and my forehead felt for the fever over and over. Nurses orders! One day as we were playing, Scooter took my face in her tiny little hands, kissed me and said, "I love you uncle Ken, I wish you were my daddy." I felt good about that for about a half second for being a good uncle but then I felt terrible about it because I was way overstepping my bounds. Scooter didn't understand the huge commitment for her that you had and that being a daddy is a whole lot more than playing patient. Besides, you are an awesome dad Keith! After Scooter said that, I backed off and did what I could so you could be with the girls. I didn't want to be the "popular" daddy taking anything away from you at all. That little event has stuck with me ever since, which made it all the more fun watching them grow up. I have tons of great memories of them as I'm sure you do since you both were and are great parents.*

*Maybe I used that memory of that story as an excuse or as a crutch but I often thought of that as Bre and Toph were growing up. It was always obvious that Patti and Lori were in a fierce struggle for attention from their parents. Lori brought it up often and Patti told me several times that Lori vied for more attention since they were little. For Lori that seemed to extend into parenting often too. Moms tend to have the easier time being the most "popular" parent, especially stay at home moms. Plus Lori seemed to want to try and make up for times when she was down and depressed. I guess that would be natural and I can understand that but it's hard to balance parenting with a spouse that seems to feel a need to be the most popular parent. Like I said, some of that is a result of my own short coming as a parent but Bre and Toph are still great kids. Having some excellent cousins to follow as examples sure helped Bre it seems. I've thanked the both of you for everything but I don't think I've ever asked you to thank them. Please do that at some point if it's appropriate.*

*My letters seem to ramble on and on about nothing sometime but it's just me writing my thoughts as they come* to mind.

    *One of the social workers asked me just this morning something that struck me funny. First she asked if she could ask me something personal. When I said yes, she asked if I would ever consider writing a book about this whole situation. My response was to ask if she was serious and why I would do that. She said that even as difficult as this whole situation is and has been, I've been holding up really well. I think what may have made her wonder that was the fact that when everything had been stripped away from me and I was feeling pretty hopeless, that same social worker had asked me what was going to keep me going. I told her that I still had a purpose to glorify God even though I had done some terrible things. Maybe she remembers that, maybe not. Don't worry. I'm not getting any delusions of grandeur about writing a book. First, I'd have to learn how to spell better and then how to write more coherently.*

    *I got another letter from [Cousin]. She's so funny. She seems just like her mom. I wrote her a while back and commented on my spelling and wondered if she would correct the letter and send it back. She didn't do that but she did put a quiz in the letter and send it back. She didn't do that but she did put a quiz in the letter with the question of when to use "your" and "you're." I guess I had misused it in the letter to her.*

    *I got a letter today from [Lawyer] saying that he will probably be here to see me on Friday. I'll see what that brings.*

    *This is most likely more than enough to read for a while so I'll let you go. I pray for you all daily.*

    *Love Ken*

# Chapter 5: The Days Following

*Dad's Letter*
*Saturday March 8, 2008*
*Dear Jan and Keith*
*Thank you so much for the pictures. It was a little hard seeing them at first in some ways but it sure lifts my heart in other ways.*
*If you will permit me, I'd like to tell you about a dream I had a couple of weeks ago. I woke up with tears in my eyes and I still get them if I think about the dream. I dreamed I was at your house, kind of like in spirit because nobody saw me. It was a Sunday afternoon before dinner and your whole family was over. A few of the girls were in the kitchen getting dinner ready and the guys helping set up or doing whatever in the living room. Bre and Toph were sitting in the living room and they seemed so <u>at peace</u>. I just lingered around, in spirit, and got to enjoy seeing the kids-Bre and Toph, "My babies" so content. Then I woke up and praised God for that dream and for the two of you.*
*I think the reason I had that dream was because I have been thinking about the kids at your house so much. A totally different scene had been worrying me for a while. I knew that Lori still wanted to marry John and it was kind of hard to think of that- Bre and Toph living with them, that is. Then on Tuesday night, January 8, one of the ladies from my divorce class at Central Wesleyan talked to me afterward. She said her teenage daughter had been going to John Doe for counseling but just told her that she would like to start seeing someone else because she didn't feel "comfortable" seeing him anymore. The prospect of Bre with John, even if it was not all that much, would have been terrible. I don't think that would have all really happened*

*but then again I didn't think Lori and John would ever do anything like what they did either.*

*I just got off the phone with mom and Ade. It's funny, they are the same as always but I appreciate them more now. I get a letter a week at least from them. It's easy to keep track of what they are up to now that I don't have my own busy life to distract me. They had just gotten home from a park program because the power went out. I though about asking if it was romantic but didn't.*

*Thanks for the note with the pictures too Jan. I like the "DeKleine 9." I know you would not have chosen this option to get from seven to nine but I am so thankful you were and are willing to take that on. Plus I know of nobody else that would do a better job with any kids. I only hear from everyone how well Bre and Toph are doing. Thank you again and sorry for how this must have screwed things up for you guys. That goes for everyone.*

*Love Ken*


*Dad's Letter*
*April 13, 2008*
*Dear Topher,*

*I love you. I'll start by saying that because I hope there is nothing wrong with that. I write "I love you" because I know that I do and I want you to know that, read that, and hear that from me and mean it with all my heart. There are so many things that I think about writing but I don't know if you are ready, if ever, to read them or if you would even want to read them. So it's kind of scary for me to write anything, but if it would let you know in a better way that I love you, I will try.*

*I think you can understand a little bit where I am coming from. It's scary sharing what's really going on inside of one's self not to mention it is sometimes very hard to put into words. When there is so much going on in my head right now it's even more difficult. There are things I want to say, things I should say, but more importantly there may be some things you want to know. If you ever have any questions of me you can just let me know. I will be as transparent as I can be and answer as openly and honestly as possible.*

*I've been thinking about what our relationship will be, can be, and should be like in the years to come. I could get really down and depressed thinking about that because we will not have opportunities to build a relationship like a normal situation, however, even if we did have, there are no guarantees that it would be perfect or great. My hope is that something I heard on the radio a while back is true and you are just like the sons that they were talking about. I think it was Dr. Dobson from Focus on the Family that said, "No matter what, son's wish they could have a better relationship with their dad." He was even talking about sons whose dad are in prison. I'm reading <u>The Secret Romance</u> right now which is a book that talks about how God is always calling us to a more intimate relationship with him and how, if we let ourself, we can hear that call in the yearning of our heart. My hope and prayer is that you will first of all hear that call from God and seek intimacy with him and that secondly you will be open to that with me too.*

*I know there are a lot of things you will have to work through before you are open or be comfortable with this but I pray that God will help you through it and that I can be whatever it is you need me to be. Please, please, please at least be open with someone. No one will have all the answers but you have a lot of wonderfully gifted people that love and care for you that will do anything they can for you. Uncle Keith and Aunt Jan have been one of my best "go to" sources for most of my life. (Aunt Jan can give you a lot of good advise about girls. You may have to ask her because she won't push it on you but it will be good advise if you ask.) I know that it may be hard for me sometimes because I'm afraid that if I say something I may look back later and think that what I said was stupid. I wish I knew just what to say and how to say it so you would hear just what you need from me. That would be great if I would just automatically know how to read your mind and then say what you most need to hear but I cannot read your mind and even if I could I may not know what to say. All I can say is that I will try with all of my heart to tell you whatever it is that you want to know or hear.*

*In my prayers I say for you every day, I ask God to give me wisdom to know to be the best dad I can be. I've done that for years but I know I slacked off on that for a time and/or just was not listening or willing to hear what God was saying. That is my responsibility to seek out, listen to, and do what God is saying so it is on me when I fail in that.*

*This is probably a really hard time for you so I would like to give you some encouragement. God has put some very wonderful people in my life that have reminded me that God loves me and is still with me. I know he has done the same for you because I hear about a lot of people that have enfolded you and Bre with so much love and kindness. My encouragement to you is to see that as God's hand reaching out to you and to know that their are a lot of people around you that are willing to let God use them to help you through this.*

*As you read this I hope that you can feel that I love you. I have a lot of things I need to work on and I would like to share some of those with you eventually or at least let you know how God is helping me through those things. It's not easy to be open and honest about anything but with some things it is especially difficult. However, by sharing how you feel about something is how you let someone get to know you. By letting someone really get to know you is how you can let them know you love them. That takes a level of trust that needs to be built up and I really want to do that with you. Actually I always have but it is a very scary thing to do and I'm not very good at it.*

  *On the lighter side, I hope your sister is being good to you. I couldn't see why she wouldn't since you are the greatest younger brother on earth. If she isn't being good to you, it sounds like you can get your big brother Kevin to stick up for you.*

  *Later Bud. I love you,*
  *Dad*

  The days immediately after the murder and confession are still in a haze- The Haze Days. It is a blur of hushed conversations, tasty casseroles, flowers, people in, people out and *Austin Powers*. Some relatives brought over the trilogy, which we binge watched with the whole crew. With everyone hollering in laughter at the simplest of jokes, we all got lost in those movies in the best way possible. My advice to anyone going through shit is not to underestimate the beautiful escape laughter can create as long as you don't turn it into a dragon to chase. Watching *Austin Powers* got me through some tough times.

  Family and friends were all in one house. It was actually pretty fun, oddly enough. We called all the helping hands "fairies"- the food fairy, the laundry fairy, the cleaning fairy; it helped lighten the mood. All these people here supporting us and helping by doing anything, whatever they could without question. This incredibly support is exactly what being a Christian is all about. If you are unwilling to clean another man's toilet, you are a nominal Christian only. My now brother, Kevin, would tell small crowds stories of when he was in college and getting into college kid shenanigans. One story that boosted my spirits was what he did with a mounted deer head. Somehow he obtained it and would go around outside of classes knocking on windows, throwing the head up and neighing like a horse. I don't think I ever told him this, but those times of laughter helped me get through the darkest moments of my life. Or the time where he was volunteering driving a bus and his fraternity brothers secretly dosed him with some X-Lax. He shat his pants and had to sit in his own excrement while driving a bus full of college kids. If I know Kevin, that seat was permanently ruined, only fire could purify that sort of filth. Classic. Sorry Kevin.

At one point I thought it would be a good idea to have my group of high school friends come over. Honestly, I didn't even want to see them but I knew I couldn't hide forever despite wanting to crawl in the nearest cave and let myself rot to death. People kept asking me when they could come by and I knew they wanted to see me. The second they came over, I wished them gone. I felt like all I could do was sit and stare at a television and had no idea what to say; I couldn't entertain these people. That's why Sitting Shiva is a thing- sometimes there is nothing to say. We got the hugs and the comforting out of the way and I quickly put in a movie so I didn't have to speak my mind, which was a ceaseless, "FUCK! SHIT! I just want to go lay in bed forever. FUCKING SHIT! FUCK! Please just end it."

I also had a lovely girlfriend at the time of the murder and began to feel the same way with her as with my friends. I couldn't entertain her; I couldn't be happy with myself let alone someone else. We were together for a lot of my mom's visitation, which consisted of nervous twirling of a water bottle in my hands while people gaped at me and felt sorry for my sad sack. There was a silent screaming plead coming from my eyes as me and my girl locked gazes and she smirked. She was great and all but I needed to let myself be sad for a while and the fear of that being contagious got to me. And so she got lost in the fray of complete reformation of my social life.

    The visitation and funeral sucked a huge mouthful of donkey dick. To anyone wondering if they should make kids go to their own parents visitation- for all that is holy, just don't. There is absolutely nothing redeeming about it for the children. It is purely emotional masturbation for everyone else; funerals are for the living, not the dead and is in no way a "healthy" part of the healing process. I hid for over half of it in the basement of the church. One of my high school teachers eventually came down to hang with me. We didn't sit there talking about emotions and bullshit. We just played Guitar Hero II and avoided the sad festival upstairs. It may be healthy to confront your problems and emotional traumas, but everyone has their own pace. I hated everything about what was happening and just wanted to play some damn Guitar Hero.

    The first five years after all this happened, my mental energy was spent on trying to convince myself life was meaningless and help wasn't necessary. Which means I got high a lot. I started out doing fine- it was just a fun thing to do every-once-and-a-while. But eventually it became too much and a few steps back was in order. My bad. Don't do drugs, kids. I was wrong about what I needed, but being wrong is necessary to figure out what is right. It took five years to realize my demons were looking for a confrontation. I sure as hell don't regret anything because personal pacing is important in times such as these.

Culture shock is something often talked about when going to new cities or countries, but the idea of it happening between families hadn't occurred to me until I moved in with my aunt and uncle. Independence was what I was used to having needed to cook and clean up after myself. My parents didn't have any rules because either they knew it wasn't necessary or didn't care. I was a good boy. Suddenly there was a curfew and all these rules to remember that had never been a part of my life. My clothes disappeared to be laundered and family dinner was mandatory attendance every night. *What is this shit? Stability?*

The first time I was late for curfew, I was writing at the coffee shop trying to finish an article for the school newspaper. Seemed like a good reason to be up late to me, so no further thought ensued. When I got home, there they were sitting at the door, wondering what I was doing and why. Despite my expressive confusion, I uttered the truth and got no punishment, but someone was waiting for me and that was a foreign concept. There was even a rule about not having a girl over when there was no adult and God forbid a bedroom door be closed. One of my friends who was a girl ended up coming over to listen to records with me while no one was home. When my aunt and uncle got home, they gave me a lecture about it. She was my friend who had a boyfriend and we were just listening to records. This just made me more confused and figured all this trouble wasn't worth it, so I stopped trying to have people over.

All of a sudden I was being told not to do drugs, have sex, watch porn, drink, stay up late. My parents never told me about any of these things so it wasn't a part of my thoughts but suddenly I curious and mixing that with being a retarded teenager I had to try some things out. Turns out they were right, all those things are just a waste of time and money. While I have no regrets because I'm the stubborn kind of ass that has to learn things for myself from experience, I would advise others not to waste their time.

With this emersion in an entirely new family culture, I quickly realized none of us knew each other. I had gone from absentee parents to overwhelming attention from people I had only seen once a year at Christmas. The shoes of biological parents are impossible to fill and I love and respect them for their effort but at the time I didn't want a substitute set, not after the failures of the first pair. No one can replace my mom- she's dead. No one can replace my father- he's alive albeit incarcerated. Am I incredibly grateful and full of love for them caring for me? Yes. But this attempt at creating a facade of a normal family life seemed too forced, unnatural, and foreign for me *at the time*.

If I had my retarded teenager way, I would have gotten an apartment by myself and tried to figure out life on my own because that's what was already happening anyway; it was comfortable for me. I was only sixteen so it's probably a good thing it didn't happen, but that is what I fantasized about at the time. I'd grown tired of all these adults telling my what to do through the divorce and the death, with everyone bickering all the time and not leaving me alone. I felt like an object being shuffled around without any say in what happened to my life. All while it was so obvious no one had their own shit together.

Things are very different now, though. Just before Ken went into the confession room he told Keith and Jan, "I did this to Lori. Now do what you do best and take care of my kids." Through writing this book and understanding why the dominoes of life fell so specifically, I have come to the conclusion that have Keith and Jan as my new parental figures is the best thing that has happened in my entire life. Take that literally. Do not underestimate the power of a strong family, a strong foundation. Abandonment of family is an abandonment of self. Throughout the years, as I made oh so many mistakes, Keith was still there waiting to give me a big ol' hairy bear hug and Jan was there doing the same- minus the hair, add a gallon bag of Puppy Chow. There is no way this life transition could have gone any better.

After the murder and the Council of House Fairies dissolved, it didn't take long to get back in the swing of normal monotony we call life. The murder happened on a Thursday and about ten days later, after exams of course, I was trying to go back to school. Being behind on school work isn't my favorite and I would have to catch up eventually so right back in I went. For a while, I thought I didn't get enough time to gather my emotions because I felt pressure from people wanted to see me get back to life. Not only is that not true but, what am I going to do, just sit around watching movies wallowing in my own sorrow? Plus school and learning is fun so it was something to focus on.

At school I was chosen to be a judge for the school talent show. I had no idea where to situate my mind around these people or how to act. *Do you guys realize life is all bullshit and this talent show no different?* Someone once told me if you don't have anything nice to say, don't say anything, so often I sat in silence. From the shifty glances I kept getting, I knew they didn't know what to do with me either. I went through the motions and acted calm and made a few jokes suppressing the existential doom looming over my head. I was trying to convince myself as much as them that I didn't feel like dying; high school in a nut shell.

Since drugs and drinking, weren't an interest yet, I took to extracurriculars. In middle school, the second I was able to do sports, I tried every single on of them. In fact, throughout high school as well, I never had an empty season, although I eventually switched to theater. I played soccer then tried out for basketball and didn't make the team, although it didn't bother me because I was only doing it out of boredom. For the winter months I dove for the swim team and in the spring I played tennis. I was average at all of these. It was an activity to kill time and get out of the house. In middle school I picked up the game of Lacrosse, which carried over until Sophomore year, the year everything happened.

All the shit happened right before Lacrosse season and just as I was beginning to train. Apathy reared it's sleepy head so I had to make up my mind on whether or not I wanted to play. I knew my decision immediately but was afraid to let my team and coach down. The head coach was an incredibly accepting and warm person. Even though he played the rough and tough lacrosse, he was always about the individual and team building. I told coach it just wasn't in the cards for me this year and made it seem like it might be a possibility next year, even though I knew it was all over. I was unnecessarily nervous when I told him I was going to try theater instead and he just smiled and said, "Okay cool!" That was that and it was done.

To the theater! The lime light wasn't the place for a sad boy so behind the scenes I went to build the set. The set guy was one of those teachers that was like a friend you didn't want to get angry. He would be the first to joke around but also the first to snap you back to reality when you need it. One time we had both the cast and crew hauling trash to the garbage and my two best friends and I got lazy and sat around while the rest of the cast was hauling lumber back and forth. We weren't really aware of what we were doing until he burst through the door and yelled, and I mean yelled, at us for being turds while the actors were doing all the hard work. He was right and we knew it right away. We grabbed our tails, shoved them between our legs, where our heads used to be, and went right to work. But ten minutes later, after the work was done and nothing else needed to be carried, we were joking and laughing like we weren't a bunch of lazy dimwits. We never admitted to how much he frightened us.

Theater was where I stayed for the remainder of high school. It is where I met two of my best friends, who are still so to this day. When I met them it was all nerves at first because they were the cool edgy theater kids and I wanted to make them my friends and so it went. The main reason being they were the only ones that weren't afraid to joke about a dead mom. All the rest of the kids were being way to nice to me and treating me like a wounded kitten. No man in his right mind wants to be treated like that. They made light and fun of my situation and that is the attitude still meant to be projected. It wasn't long before they invited me to the local misfit coffee shop to hang out with the freaks and geeks. I picked up the habit of smoking a pipe, which was a pretty big deal at the time because I was only seventeen and it made me feel like a badass. We went to thrift stores to get Acapulco shirts and cure boredom. If we weren't bumming around the coffee shop, we were sitting in Denny's smoking peach flavored Cheyennes, drinking dirt coffee and eating greasy things until the cows came home.

Some times we would get into some subtle mischief. They wanted to do a senior prank and, even though I was just a junior, I was invited to join. We found an old Mr. Rogers posters we considered a shrine to the holy man himself, RIP. We devised a rig which made the poster fall from the ceiling in the middle of a school chapel. We thought long and hard about it and didn't want to ruin any sort of religious festivity so we did it during an awards ceremony no one took seriously anyway. We also didn't want to cause havoc or extra work for Bob the janitor, our pal. All we wanted was confusion for the general population. Bob ended up complimenting us later on our creativity and thanking us for not doing something destructive. We set up a timer under the stage that would play the Mr. Rogers theme at a precise time. Since we were genius little bastards and already had people suspecting us of something, we set up a decoy speaker with a blank CD labeled "Project Manhattan." It worked splendidly; the chapel runner fell right into our trap and thought he foiled our plan. We also knew we wouldn't be able to miss out on attendance so we hired alumni goons to do the dirty work. One curtain man to pull it up when the music started, two people launching homemade T-shirts with Mr. Rogers' face on it, and a getaway driver. It all went pretty well, although the curtain didn't open all the way so only about half the audience saw the poster and the other half was just confused, which is all we wanted anyway. The music started blaring and the teacher on stage looked around confused before dancing an Irish jig. I was up in the tech booth operating the cameras with the chapel runner to whom I confidently turned my head, locked eyes and smirked the smirkiest smirk smirkable. He looked around franticly because that was his job and he was so confident he put a stop to our schemes. We got a few laughs and everyone went about the normal day. Since the people in charge knew it was us and it was still considered a prank, we were all called to the principal's office. The principal was cool about it and admitted what he was doing was only did because he had to. He thanked us for not doing anything destructive and not ruining a serious assembly. Since he had to give us a punishment, he made it light; vacuum the library after school, a task that took forty-five minutes- a very smiley and arrogant forty-five minutes.

    One year a couple of our friends got hit by a car on their bikes. One of them sustained brain injuries and passed due to medical complications, while the other was severely injured. A few days after the accident, five of my friends and I convened at Denny's and talked about it over Cheyennes and coffee. The injured one was a fan of a comedy radio show called Free Beer and Hot Wings, whose studio was in Grand Rapids, a mere thirty minutes away. We decided on two things: to buy him the last Radiohead vinyl, completing his collection, and get the guys from Free Beer and Hot Wings to visit.

    Since the show aired really early we decided to pull an all-nighter and make it to the studio by five in the morning. We killed time at Denny's- a lot of time- trudged to the studio, sat outside and waited for one of them to come into work. We ended up finding one of the hosts as he was coming into the studio and surrounded him in an innocent mob. He later said he was gripping his moped helmet, ready to hit us because we were five guys ambushing him. Fortunately he didn't react that way and our elected spokesperson explained the situation while we all just stared like idiots. Our representative said our friend was in and accident, which the host had heard and immediately knew what we were talking about. We said the hospitalized fellow was a big fan and would love it if they came to visit him at any point. Host guy, being a chivalrous gentleman, immediately agreed and said he would talk to the other guys for us. We exchanged numbers on the spot while he affirmed he would call us after the show wrapped at ten. We got some hot dogs for breakfast and took naps in shifts while parked at a Wal-Mart. Within a few minutes of the show finishing, we got the call. After meeting at the studio, they all followed us in their respective vehicles: a racing striped Corvette and a moped.

A procedure had just concluded so we ended up having to wait for a half hour of awkward silence in the hallway. Thankfully the patient wasn't too doped up and recognized them right away. The radio guys ended up giving him their card and a bunch of swag, then invited him to attend an Omelette Friday with a guest of his choice, which he ended up doing with his dad after he recovered. That night is one of the most memorable experiences of my life. Not only was it fun on a surface level but it made me feel deeply happy and we are all in contact to this day.

Despite having to reevaluate my entire existence, it really all does work out in time. It's easy to focus on the bad things right after it happens, but eventually you learn how to enjoy things again. Occasionally life will remind me what happened, but it's only a problem if you let it be. Some times when people go through their own shit and look to me for support and advice, I get flashbacks of my own history and can't help but selfishly shrink away because there is nothing to say. It's never something that's caused real problems, but still something of which to be conscious and aware. Wounded hearts wound hearts. As the wise sage, Pumbaa, so eloquently declares, "You gotta put your behind in the past."

*Dad's Letter*
*Sunday March 30, 2008*
*Dear Bre and Christopher,*
  *I hear from so many people that you each are doing very well in everything you are doing. Christopher, I am so*

*glad for several different reasons that you did not go out for Lacrosse. I hated to think of you getting injured and messing up plans you had for later on in life. I'm really glad that you made the decision yourself and didn't just go out for the team for me or anybody else. I know [Coach] thought a lot of you and was looking forward to having you on the team next year but if it's not your interest anymore I'm cool with that and I'm sure he is too. If you are wondering, he may know you enough for him to say he was looking forward to having you on the team, I know he told me once that he had heard some really good things about you from teachers. Now I am very glad to hear that you went out for the play and then stayed with theater by working on the set.*

*Bre, I heard so many compliments on "Showcase" and Living Hope* (school singing show and group, respectively.) *[Your cousin] sent me a bunch of pictures of Showcase. I cannot imagine how you can do so well and seem to enjoy being up there performing so much. It has always been so natural for you. I used to get all nervous for you when you would have a performance but you made that go away by always doing it so joyfully that I could just feel your joy fill my heart.*

*Well guys, it is so great to hear about so many wonderful things the two of you are doing or having happen. Everyone I hear from says the two of you are being such a blessing to so many people. I get cards and letters from family, friends, and people from church that say you are both doing amazingly well. That is a real answer to prayer. In the normal living of life I never prayed for the two of you like I do now. God seems to have answered my prayers because in spite of me and the shitty life situations you have had to live through and have both chosen to do the best you can do. And you are doing very well.*

*I want to say that I am sorry for all my part of making the both of you live through some deep crap. Saying "sorry" is such a small thing but I hope you will allow me to start there. There is so much and so many things that I feel I need to say I'm sorry for. I only hope my doing that will help you in some way. I battle in my mind so much about what to say or write to you because I wonder what would do you the most good.*

*Someday maybe you will be able to forgive me for all of my pride. I'm starting to see how my pride has gotten in the way of having good and true relationships with you both and with so many other people. I'm sure the both of you can think of several times when I was too proud to say I was wrong. But, there is good pride too and I am very proud of the both of you. I hope you keep living your lives the way you are and keep glorifying God with your lives. I love you both so very much and it hurts to think about you sometimes. It would be easier to distract myself and not think about "what could have been", but I want to encourage you and tell you I love you. It's hard for me to write to you both because I don't know if you will ever want to hear from me. Just know that I love you and will respect what ever way you feel toward me. I can't imagine what it's like to be in you shoes. You had a father that, for a long time, always wanted to be right. Now I'm learning since I'm far from perfect that in order to be right I have to admit to being wrong sometimes. I was very wrong sometimes but didn't want to admit it. I hope you can take all those grains of sand you have had in your lives, make like a clam and turn that sand into pearls...*

I love you guys!
Love Dad

*Dad's Letter*
*Sunday March 30, 2008*
  *Dear Keith,*
  It was so great to get your card! Hearing about all the fun stuff going on at your house makes me unbelievably happy for the kids. I knew they would thrive in your family and would see a whole new world open up to them. But more importantly, I think they will be able to view their world from an entirely different perspective. By different I mean realistic, factual yet loving, and not in a "poor me" victim mentality. To hear about everything they are doing makes my heart soften and makes me praise God for how He is blessing them so.
  There is an element that makes me extremely sad. Like when I think of all the things I am missing from day to day. I seem to be missing those things more and more. What's worse is when I think of all the things in the future that I will miss. I try to stay away from that and just take it a day at a time. On the other hand, I love to hear that the kids "just seem to like it at home." I knew right away that they would like to be home more soon after they got settled in. Once they got comfortable they would get past all the crap Lori was feeding them about you guys and everyone else associated with me. I can't tell you enough how thankful I am to have you.
  I did have a good Easter. A big reason for that was because I knew the kids would have a great time. I remember Easter last year very well. Bre and Toph come over with your whole family then too. That was wonderful for me last year and now that Bre and Toph are part of the DeKleine 9, I'm sure they had even a better time.
  I guess you have figured out that I think the world of your family. Toph just has to be so happy in order for him to be doing all this new stuff. I could tell so clearly that he

was miserable when he had to be at home on Calvin Ave. It might not be as obvious with Bre but I imagine she has a calmer spirit about her too. Well, maybe just a little since she can get too many plates spinning in the air at times. Nonetheless, I'm sure she is happy.

Maybe I'm trying to make a justification for my actions way too much. I don't want to think that the kids are better off now if there is not any truth to that. Only they can answer that with their limited knowledge and understanding. I do think they had no idea what they were going to be up against in the years to come with Lori. On the other hand I'm trying to figure out how and to what extent I short-circuited in this situation too. (I'm sure there are some people that would love to tell me. Some have.)

Thank you both for making my dream for Bre and Toph a reality. That is the Sunday afternoon dream but also much more than that.

There is one thing that I want to tell someone and I hope you can understand a little bit. I'm making head way or getting a little better at something here over the last month. I had asked [someone] to send me one of the Memorial Service announcements and I got it about a month ago. I didn't know there was a picture on it. I still have it but for a long time, when ever I saw the picture, I would get so angry. It was just so automatic. Not so much at Lori but more at the things she was doing. Now I understand more of how and why John was putter her up to so many of the things but I was still just getting *so* angry. I thank God some of that is subsiding. I pray so hard everyday for God to help me with that.

I plan to try writing another letter to Bre and Christopher that I actually send to you. Just hang on to it until the time when and if they are ever ready to read it.

Love you all

*Ken*

# Chapter 6: Planted Seeds and Inspired People

*Mom's Journal*
*No Date*
*The other day someone came knocking on my front door.*

*There he was at my front door. He said he was seventeen and that he and his dad had just moved up from Arkansas. That at least explained his slight hillbilly accent. His hair was a bit disheveled, his attire moderately messy- loose jeans, a somewhat wrinkled oxford-like shirt. I don't remember his feet. He said that tomorrow was his dads birthday and that he wanted to buy him a present, so if there was "anything" he could do, like mow the "la-awn" or "somethin'." "I'm a real hard worker." My first response was to get rid of him. He was probably a druggy looking for some quick cash for a quick fix- but oh man- I'm a sucker. Something spoke to my little selfish brain, you know the one that says maybe he is for real and "Oh this is so sad." So I started exploring him.*

*I said, "Ya know, there are a lot of things you could do for your dad for his birthday that don't cost anything."*
*"Yaw, I know, but I really wanna give him sum'thin'."*
*"Oh. Well if you could buy him something, what would you get him?"*
*"Oh, I dunno, a watch or somethin'."*
*My mind raced to earlier that week when I was cleaning my house. I had purchased a 2-watch set at Kmart cheap cheap cuz one of the watches is what Toph was looking for. I remember looking at the other watch*

*thinkin'*, "Now what the heck am I gonna do with this thing? It's too big for me. Toph likes the other watch and Bre isn't the least bit interested in it. So I just let it lie.

"A watch, really?! Wait just a second."

I darted back into the house thinking surely that God had meant for this to happen and the boy would bubble with joy and be thankful beyond words.

"Here ya go! It's yours" I said, feeling that surely heaven was watching all this. I told him it was brand new, never warn, perfect condition.

"Wow, y'all got some cologne to go with thayt?"

I suppose I could have been indignant but I prefer to cherish pity, lest I drive an angel from my door.

*Dad's Letter*
*Wednesday September 3, 2008*
*Dear Keith,*

Bre is off to Calvin today and Toph started his junior year! Wow, I probably know more than what you do about what what she is going to be doing this weekend and for the next several months. Calvin has not changed a whole lot with what they do for freshmen since I was there twenty-seven years ago. A few years ago someone told me what they did as freshmen after they moved in and it was pretty much the same orientation, dorm activities, registration, upper class men moving in, and of course figuring out cafeteria. I'm sure Bre is having a riot. Saturday night is usually a freshmen talent show where all the guys like to go to check out the freshmen girls before they got DBD (Dutch Butt Disease). I can so see Bre doing something in the talent sow.

I keep saying a blessing on Bre and Toph everyday, and for you and Jan too. There is not much I can do from here but I can do that so I keep doing it.

*I want to tell you about something that happened today. I was taken out of my cell and walked (escorted) by an officer over to another building for a dental check up. As we were walking I thanked the officer for treating me with respect even though he knew nothing about me. He had walked me somewhere else before, and I had seen him with other prisoners, and he was very kind with everyone (most of them are). After I thanked him, he said that he always figured, "But for the grace of God go I." He said he could very well be in a prisoners shoes now if his life had been different and like some of ours. I didn't tell him but I remembered that I made a point of thinking that same thing as I left the booking area at HPD. As I punched my number in the key pad for exiting booking after I had dropped someone off after arresting them, I would say, "But for the grace of God go I."*

*At first this afternoon I thought that I cannot say that anymore. Even with the grace of God, I have gone where, and forever will be where, I thought the grace of God had kept me from and always would keep me from. That really bummed me out and I was very down until I thought about it some more tonight. I realized I still have the grace of God because I still have hope. I will never be free again and out of prison but I am and I will be free in another way. Not only that but I still have a loving family and friends who care for me. A lot of guys here do not have anything like that. Because of that I still have something to be thankful for. With that I still have hope that I can be some good for someone in the future.*

*I'm told that my time here at Jackson will be the worst time ever. I'm in a 6x9 ft cell and there is nothing to do. I have not been able to get a Bible yet and I don't know if I ever will. No TV, no books, nobody to talk to. I was thrilled yesterday to get my store order and get this paper and pen. I started writing letters right away. I'm doing well in spite of having nothing to do. I surprise myself at how well I can adapt to these circumstances. Three days ago I started doing something to keep my mind occupied. I started thinking of all of my oldest memories on the farm. Once I got started I was shocked at some of the things that come to mind. The more I thought about it the more I remembered. As I laid here thinking, without any distractions, I thought of memories that I have not had for twenty to thirty years. I took each building on the farm and thought of my earliest memory of it. Once I got started I kept doing that for hours. Sometime laughing at the things I thought of. Like that old brown teddy bear I had. Or was that yours? Eventually the left eye was missing. I started writing all those memories down and after twelve pages I was only done with the hatchery and the old chicken coop.*

*After I thought through all the buildings I went through a bunch of other topics like vacations, holidays, relatives, reunions, jobs, special events and so on. If I could write it all down it would be a couple hundred pages. I'll see how far I get. It sure is fun to think of all that stuff. Memories come flooding out when you put them in context, with something. Especially if you have the time to do it.*

September 5, 2008

*I got mail today! A short letter and two letters with Catholic information from an old couple I knew from Glenn. They have sent me all kinds of information about the Venerable Solanus Casey, Capuchin. They are part of a guild that is trying to get Friar Casey Sainted. I don't understand how all that works but it is interesting.*

*I talked with a former cop from Livingston a few days ago and a prosecutor from Malcolm County today while I had my "yard time." It looks like we will all be going to*

*Ionia. I have no idea what they are here for. I have not been able to talk to them much. What I mean by "yard time" here is when an officer escorts us to a small enclosed area outside where we are safe from everyone else. So don't worry. I'm safe. Food is better here and you get more. Plus I got a pen! I've been sleeping great here too. Eight hours straight through.*

*I imagine you will be starting at the farm soon again. I'll miss that. It was so much fun going out there with you and working like fools for four weeks. I'm so glad I got to do that at least once.*

September 9, 2008

*I received three letters from you yesterday. You did a lot of writing in order to get me caught up on everything. Thank you much! It will be a set of letters I will read over and over again. It will give me something to respond to also. I usually go through each letter I get from people and circle the things I'd like to comment to.*

*Yes your letters did find me OK as you had hoped. In fact I'm probably doing even better than that. A different Social Worker/Psych person just came by to check on me today just as I sat down to write you. He actually talked for a few minutes instead of just asking if I was OK and moving on. He asked if I had a Bible and I had to tell him not yet. He explained that it might take a while. Then he stayed and talked for several minutes, I told him about my background and he said he was Seventh Day Adventist. I would have liked to talk to him a long time but eventually he had to move on. That was/will be a highlight of my day.*

*Yes I imagine that the 25th* (The Trial) *was difficult for you and everyone in the family on friends of mine/ours. I was pretty well set for it so I just went through the motions. I for sure didn't pay much attentions to what Lori's parents or sister said.*

*I imagine it is an issue on whether or not something should have been said to the media. I know that the differences can and will be dealt with and I hope and pray that it's not too much of a problem. I just wish that I could have been more in the loop of communication in figuring that out beforehand but as it was there had to be too much second guessing. If I had known that Bill would not be saying anything I would have prepared to say a few things to the "public" at sentencing. One thing I would have said for sure would have been to thank everyone who supported the kids, our family, and me. That has been greater than I ever could have thought possible. Another thing I would like to have communicated is that I'm thankful that it looks like John Doe will to be able to do this to anyone else and that I hope people become more aware of the possibility of these types of things happening. But, it didn't work out that way and there was not way for me to have known that far enough in advance.*

*As for the decision not to have [Brother] say anything to the media, I would put the most stock in what Bre actually thinks and says. Her and Toph are the ones that, more than anyone, have to deal with Lori's family. Like [a friend] told me, "All you can do is pray that God guards their minds against anything Lori's family says." Without Bre or Toph being at the sentencing some things could have tactfully been said indirectly to Lori's parents that will probably have to be said sooner or later. They have no real idea what Lori had been like for so many years because for so long they were so out of touch. Our family dealt with Lori more than hers did by far. Like I said, I'll respect Bre's choices for much of this because of knowing where she is coming from. She doesn't know all of the dynamics of the situation but she and Toph are in the middle of dealing with* them.

 *In all that I respect your choice to ask [Brother] not to say anything at that point. You said you could understand some of where he is coming from and so can I. Yes, part of the motivation for saying something was maybe out of anger but I don't think that came across too strongly and some of that is OK too. Knowing Lori's parents as I do, I will be surprised if they do not keep pushing certain issues on their agenda and they will have to be addressed for that sooner or later.*

 *I entrusted Bre and Toph to you and Jan for a reason. That is because I knew you would love Bre and Toph and always do everything for them that you think is in their best of interest. I don't expect perfection but I know everything will be done in love. Anyone that knows you and Jan will know that about you. However, even things done in love for Bre and Toph can be used against you and I think that Lori's parents will do just that. I know this because now I've experienced that from them and will expect it again for you. For instance or example, here is something they would pull. They will really push for something they want to do for or with Bre and Toph when it doesn't work out for you or is against your better judgement for them to do it. If you make an issue of it, you're screwed. If you let it go they will say you don't care enough about them and you are screwed that way too. They did nothing but give me rock and hard place situations to be in since I got back from Iraq or just after.*

 *The biggest reason I'm trying to explain this is that I have no knowledge of you and Jan ever having to deal with someone like this before. Jan's folks certainly are not that way and I don't see that in our family. After having tried to explain some of that, I'll say that I'll trust the wisdom of you and Jan in how to handle it the best way possible. In* last talking to [brother] I told him of this/my concern of Lori's parents steamrolling everyone to get what they want. He agreed. (There's a reason their family never had anything to do with them.) Hopefully I'm giving you a heads up and that will be enough. One of the reasons I did not take John Doe's life and then my own was that I wanted to ensure that Bre and Toph were entrusted to you and Jan. I'm still very glad I did that.

You mentioned Bre saying that she wanted to write a letter of thanks to the community after the [Policemen vs. Fireman Baseball Fundraiser] game on September 1. Do you know if that happened at all? I hope she did but I also know that this is one of the ways she would get out of something- put it off until she can't do it or it's too late. That's my girl! I love her like crazy for it.

I'm looking forward to hearing more from you about what worked out for the better with nothing being said to the media on our part. You said you and Jan went to breakfast with [friend]. On [brother's] recommendation I did write [friend] a letter on August 26. He has been one of the hardest ones for me to communicate with. He is the best and maybe that's why it's more difficult.

Topher sure gets his mind set on things doesn't he? So it's saltwater fish now huh? If it's not one things it's another with that boy. I give him a lot of credit. He always amazed me how goal oriented he is. Once he gets it in his head, that becomes a huge focus for him. Not an obsession but he just must think about it a lot and works toward his goal whenever he gets a chance. That is great. I just wish he had time to do everything he has always wanted to do. Does he still have his electric guitar? He worked and saved like crazy for a while to but it but I don't think he ever was able to do anything with it. The interest soon faded. At least he went after his interest and gave it a try. If I thought about *saltwater fish, I'd right away think of how expensive they are, how much work it is, and how hard they are to keep alive. Oh well, it will be another good learning experience for him. Maybe that's why he's so smart.*

*Fay Key, yes she is a hoot. I can very well imagine what that was like. She has so many interesting stories and she would tell you all of them if you gave her the chance. Her cat that she named Dawg died a few years ago. She has always been a sweetheart to me. It's good to stay in touch with her now.*

*That is so great that [brother's and a friend] took Toph fishing up north. I'm just thrilled to hear that. Even if they didn't catch much I'm sure they had fun. That's right up Toph's alley.*

*So Bre eventually got off to Calvin on September 3. I bet that was a process! What futon did [Bre's Friend] pick up from storage? The only one I know of is the one that I had in the house. If that's the one I'm glad she took it. Bre is in Rooks! That's Rooks/VanDellen dorm. [College roommate] and I lived in the guys side of that dorm for two years. It's so nice for me to know just where she's living and what she is going through. That was nice to read about Bre putting the rock from Pictured Rock by Lori's grave too. I'm sure Bre and Toph are making a lot of happy memories now. Have they been able to get together with [their new cousins] at all since the trip up north? Maybe Bre can have them come to Calvin for a weekend and sleep on the futon.*

*Well I have somewhat of a mirror now. Man! Is my head ever gray! I haven't been able to shave for a while here and this is the first time I can see myself. I kind of like it and may keep the beard if I can trim it up some.*

*September 9*

*I got a letter from Mom and [sister] today. I have a*

*bunch of letters written but I have no way to get it out to anyone. I don't know when I'll be able to call anyone again either. Everyone's letters keep getting longer and longer. I'll respond to mom and [sister's] letters too in hopes that I can get them out soon.*

*September 15*
*You are finally getting a letter because I finally got envelopes to mail letters out with. Thanks for stopping in and talking with [a friend] too. She has been great through all of this. I'm getting mail from most of the regulars again as of last week. Thanks for getting my address out. Oh yea, [that friend] said you are a great guy. I told her I already knew that but I would pass it on.*
*Love you all*
*Ken*

Monkey see, monkey do. Many of my dad's friends and family stuck by his side since the very beginning. I never knew how many friends he had until he went to prison. Many have visited him over the years and still visit him regularly. These people amaze me and I would like to thank all of them for having his back and adhering to their principles which have inspired me to check and ask myself if I could do the same thing. Eventually I realized there was only one way to find out: dive in and go for a swim.

Ken's brother, my Uncle Keith says he never could say anything defending my father because people knew his bias all too well and figured no one would listen. He was Ken's brother, not Lori's and sides were assumed during the divorce, murder, and trial. This situation is beyond him versus her, though. Sure he is going to look like he is on my dad's side because he visits, sends pictures, and the like, but it is much more layered and complicated than that and there is compassion for both sides on his part. No one will listen to anyone but me or my sister on the subject because we are the obvious "victims" and if I can forgive him, no one else has an excuse. Now, don't get me wrong, there were many people massively affected, but we are very arguably affected the most. My aunt and uncle always would frequently have people ask them, "How are the kids?" To which they would reply, "*We* are all doing fine, thank-you."

Keith played a huge role in my perspective shift. The key thing: he let it ride. I never felt pressure to interact with my dad, making each step I took self driven. He told me he knew I'd get there eventually, but until then, silence was the name of the game. Letters were gathered and stored until I was ready as well as reminding me he never told my dad about anything I did, because he wanted that to be my decision and my task. Although, other family members kept Ken up to date, which I don't blame them for at all. All this time, Keith was one of the few in understanding and continuing to love my father. Sure Ken had friends that would visit, but very little intermingling was done, due to what, I do not know for sure. I think all his visitors were afraid of what people in a small Christian community would think if everyone knew they were visiting a murderer.

When I told Keith I wanted to write this book, Pandora's Box opened and we began to talk a lot more about this whole mess. He told me that he had a lot of things built up; things he couldn't tell people and it was very therapeutic to finally release his bottled thoughts. In times and circumstances such as these, it's hard to trust anyone with all the sour information. But silence can speak volumes and sometimes the best way to change the world is through cooperation, not intimidation and it has been a very positive bonding experience for the both of us.

The new family situation caused many unique relationships to incur. My aunt and uncle were now my parent replacements. Are they my new parents? No, that's not what they are; I have parents even if they aren't present. Are they my guardians? No, that sounds stale and they're much more than that. What do I call it then? Probably doesn't matter. I received love and I continue attempting to give it back.

Ken has many friends still visiting him. The names I will not divulge, but you know who they are and I would like to say thank you. Thank-you for sticking in it for my dad. Thank you for showing me what love is. Thank you for doing something most people are afraid to do. You are brave. You are kind. You are love and are loved. I forgot the name of that ancient hippy who hung out with prostitutes and criminals. Oh wait, that was Jesus. "He that is without sin among you, let him first cast a stone" and all that.

*Dad's Letter*
*Tuesday Feb 19, 2008*
*Dear Friend, Mrs. Fay Key,*
*Thank you for remaining a faithful friend. It means a lot to get cards and letters. Hearing what is going on in the life of friends is always nice to keep up with and encouraging. My life doesn't change very much right now so there is not a lot to write about from my end.*

*One thing I do like to share with people that I write is that I am having a great time reading through entire books of the Bible in one sitting. Either I have never had the time or never took the time to read more than a few chapters at a time. Now I have large blocks of time to read and reread. Plus there are no distractions to steal my attention or nothing pressing on my mind of something else I could be doing. Reading the whole book of Genesis in one afternoon gives it more of a meaning that I ever knew.*

*This cannot make me or anyone else any better than we were before but I know it doesn't hurt. I know that there is nothing I can do to make God love me more and there is nothing I can do to make God love me less. The same goes for all of us and all we have to do is accept that from Him. I guess that is hat theologians call Grace.*

*Another thing I am enjoying is actually writing letters again. The last time I wrote letters was while I was in Basic Training in Georgia during 1988. You reminded me that letter writing is still one of the better ways to communicate even when there are phones and email.* **Your passion for letters I have not forgotten but I don't think anyone will be putting together a book about letters from prison. On the other hand, maybe someone will since there are books out there about all kinds of other things.**

*I hope your family is well. You pray for my family so I will do the same for yours. From what I hear both my kids - Bre, 18 and Chris, 16- are doing well. Since they are with my brother's wonderful family, my son is now planning on going to college locally instead of going as far away as he could get. He sees now what a functional mother's home is like and realizes how nice having family around can be. He wants to remain a part of that.*

*I have envelopes that I can mail directly to you now. I wrote several letters and sent them to [a friend], and asked him to bring them to a few people. Yours was included in there. I hope he brought it to you a couple weeks ago.*

*Than you again Sister Gene!*
*God Bless You,*
  *Love Ken*

*Dad's Letter*
*Tuesday August 5, 2008*

*To my dear Friend Fay Key,*

*I am so glad that you were able to talk to my mom. I have not heard from her since last Friday but I'm sure she will let me know about it in her next letter. I have always liked to get two people that don't know each other, but I know and care about, connected. Especially you and my mother. I think the both of you have a lot in common but you may have figured that out already. You may really enjoy reading the story of my step-dad. He wrote it about ten years ago and it covers the time in his life when he lived in occupied Netherlands until after he became and Engineer on Merchant Marine ships in the Pacific during WWII. I found it very interesting. It's all in his own hand writing which adds character to it. It's 130 plus pages.*

*You have asked several times if there is anything that you can do or wrote that you wished there was something you could do for me. I thought of something yesterday that you may want to consider doing. Yesterday I was finishing up reading a book called "The Prayful Spirit: Passion for God/Compassion for People" by James P. Gills, MD. Dr. Gills writes about how prayer has changed his life, his practice, and the lives of several of his patients. As I was reading the book I thought of how good it would be for my son Chris to get and read this book too since he wanted to be a doctor. The book has several stories from other doctors of how God has affected them too. I'm sure you would like the book also and after reading it, you could pass it on to Chris. This week he is working at Camp Sunshine, north of Holland, helping with handicapped kids that they have come for the week. I'm sure that will be a learning and growing experience for him. Bre did it last year and really enjoyed it. Anyway, that was a thought I had in case that would be something you would like to do.*

*I'm glad you had a great time at your birthday party.*

*It sounds like you had it at a great place. I always love the beach on Lake Michigan. You said in your letter before that you joked about wearing a bathing suite there but that you had never worn one before so why would you start at eighty-seven. Am I to assume that you never wore anything at all when you went swimming then? Ha Ha. Your party must have been a good time to remember all people and experiences you have been blessed with. For the first part of our lives we often look ahead on our birthdays but after a while we use the time of our birthdays to look back. However, with some unique people like yourself, the other people you've affected look back at your life and look to the future and hope you have many more years yet to come. I am one of those people that hopes you have many more years.*

 *You asked if I am treated well. Yes the guards are very good to me and respect me as much as I would hope for. They are very good with everyone, or at least most try to be, but some of the inmates make it very difficult for them. As for being safe with other inmates, I don't have any contact with anyone yet other than one guy by the name of Jay. We get to see each other through a door for a few hours each day is all. We get along well and have been reading the Bible some or praying. I am completely safe and have no problems with anyone.*

 *You have mentioned that your two sons had to spend some time in prison before. I don't know what for, nor do I need to know, but it sounds like they are doing alright now.*

 *Wherever I end up, I'll probably be in protective custody I am told. I don't know what that means but I'm sure they have had situations like this before. I don't know where I'll end up but my family or I will let you know.*

 *Visits are very limited at this point and are only a half hour once a week and very early on Friday, Saturday or*

*Sunday mornings. If my family visits they can give me updates on Bre and Toph or anyone else so most all of my visits have been family.*

*Everyone started calling my son Chris by a nickname of Toph a few years ago. It comes from Chris-TOPH-er and he likes it so if I refer to Toph, I'm talking about my son.*

*Yes you may like to talk a lot but at least you have something to say. Some people I've known like that like to talk a lot but don't have anything I care to hear about so there is a big difference. I got a good laugh at the T-shirt that says, "Help- I'm talking and I can't shut up."*

*I'm glad you liked our plans of hiking the Grand Canyon. If you have a map of it at all maybe you can find where we can hike down to the Colorado River from the South Rim. We can start on the Kaibab Trail going down. The trail head is a few miles east of where the main visitors area is for the National Park. On the Kaibab Trail it's seven miles down to the river with several switchbacks on the trail because of the steep sides you have to go down. The view is beautiful everywhere you look so you have to stop and look around some because if you are walking you need to keep your eyes on the trail. Not that you would risk falling off a cliff but you wouldn't want to risk tripping. Once we get down to the river we can follow it down stream to Phantom Ranch. It's a little coral for trail mules where we can get water bottles filled up, have lunch, and make a phone call from the bottom of the Grand Canyon if you want. Then we can start hiking up the Bright Angle Trail. That trail is nine miles long from Phantom Ranch up to the rim. About half way up we can take a break at the Bright Angle campground which is in a beautiful green garden oasis along the trail. The rest of the way up has a lot of switch backs on the trail again with a few small tunnels to go through because it gets to be a steep way up.*

*The trail is very walkable but when one considers it's a mile from the rim down to the river and a mile back up again, it's quite a day hike. It takes some getting in shape to do it in one day but one day could last a long time in heaven. I've always wanted to take my whole family and several friends there and in heaven I'll be able to do that. Then you can take me to the Everglades!*
  *Until next time. Thanks for your care and concern.*
    *Love Ken*


    Fay Key is an elder woman who lived on my dad's police beat in Holland and became one of his best friends while he would frequently visit her on duty to stop and chat. As you can tell by the letter, they became close friends and even planned their Grand Canyon trip once they get to visit each other in Heaven.
    Fay Key is about ninety-five years old now but is as spry and clever as a fox on Adderall. When you visit her, there is a good chance she will be walking her laps around the house, climbing a tree (which got her in trouble with her kids), or writing poetry and is the kind of person that doesn't get sick because she doesn't believe in it. Those are her words and she is not wrong; she told me she hasn't been sick- not even a cold- in 30 years. On the matter she also said, "You hold life and death on the tip of your tongue. You can speak negative until the air is completely full of negativity. We don't see it bouncing around- you can't slap it like fly. But if that's what you spit out into the air, that's what you are going to be living with."
    I could write a whole other book on her life and personality but she has done that already in her published book *My Life in Bits and Pieces*. She is also a published poet, where she writes about herself because, in her words,

"That's all I know about." Her and my dad were and are BFF's and have been in touch while he was in prison via pen and post. Fortunately for me, she kept all the letters in a neatly organized binder like I used to do with Pokemon cards. "I've got all his letters that he wrote me", she said. "I don't know if that will help you." Yup. Although she wanted me to use photocopies of his handwritten letters. That'd be neat and all, but I know his handwriting and not even a pharmacist on the Adderall he prescribed that fox could decipher such a linguistic nightmare.

    When I first talked to her, she mentioned she wanted to write a book with all the letters, but it didn't feel right. Then when I told her what I was doing, she immediately gave up the letters and said I was the one that needed to be doing this. Also yup. Sounds like someone else I know. Although it has been many years since I've seen her, she is a true joy and inspiration and I've learned a lot from our conversations; some of which she let me record.

    Little Fay was born in 1921 Arkansas, where she was raised with a few brothers and sisters by her parents on a farm. She always spoke highly of her father and is not afraid to admit that she likes men better than women although she will also admit prejudices and never fully commit to the statement. She has been through multiple husbands. One of them turned out to be a bigamist who had another family; the other was an alcoholic who killed himself in a drunken car accident. "He died the way he lived", she says. She birthed seven kids from the second asshole and raised them all by herself in Holland, Michigan. She still lives in the same house, a house filled with "enough junk to fill all the trash bins in the world. And it is junk… I just keep stuff."

    Also she is a talker, which is a vast understatement. She will ramble until you can't listen anymore, then continue on even as you walk out the door and start your car. The first visit I had with her, she spoke for three hours straight; the second visit, more than that. She won't ever make a statement without a disclaimer and verbally second guessing herself. It's not that she is self-conscious, just incredibly self-aware. She'll say she doesn't like a certain kind of person, then admit to the fallacy of her prejudice.

    The first time I went to visit her was almost exactly five years to the day after the murder. She had written me letters and birthday cards over the years, but I never replied because I thought this was just some crazy old coot that happened to like my dad. Since I had never contacted her, she knew nothing about me or what I looked like, other than what my father had said in his letter and I didn't call before I went to her house because I wanted to surprise her. She definitely wanted to speak to me based on conversations with Keith, as well as the fact she sent me a bunch of letters over the years.

    Fay's house is near the downtown area so I parked around the corner and strolled on over. When I drove past her house, she was outside picking up leaves and trash with her bare hands out in the bitter cold. I walked up to the front door in the arctic wind and knocked a few times with my numb knuckles. No answer. I figured she was old and hard of hearing, which she later verified. I knocked harder and my fist began to hurt so I started to doubt if this was even going to happen. A fresh batch of letters ready to be sent were peaking out her mailbox. After a couple more impatiently hard knocks, she came to the door.

    She looked confused but curious and told me the front door did not open and I should go around back, still with a look of confusion. I eagerly walked to the back door which she then opened for me. When she opened the door she didn't say anything so I said, " Hello, my name is

Christopher DeKleine and that I believe you knew my father." Immediate tears and hug along with a touch of euphoric exasperation.

Through cut-off sentences and flustered gasps, I was invited in. She started talking about how long she had waited for this day and how overjoyed she was that it had finally come to fruition. Not only was I happy to oblige her dream, it had been one of mine to meet her for quite some time now. Immediately she starting talking about my dad: how he started to come and listen to her while she talked, how they wrote back and forth while he was in Iraq. Nothing but love, love, love. "You know Chris", she starts, "There's not any reason, there's not anything you could figure out- a psychiatrist, a psychologist, or any 'All-ja-mologist' (chuckles) that could tell me why I loved that man. He was kind. He was here to help us... I think there was a bond there. If anything that I could say to him, or a letter I could write him, would cheer him up for thirty seconds, that's all I could ask for." *I'm just as confused as you are, lady.* He would come by at least once a week and "We'd sit here and he'd listen. He was very quiet. I don't know why he would come by because he never got to say nothing. I used to offer him coffee but he would never even have coffee."

Hearing about all her tragedies and how she dealt with them was eye opening. She had been treated like dirt by all these people but didn't hold an ounce of resentment. "You can't deny you got a father out there, you know" she says, "You can not be happy with him or be very unhappy with him. But he's there and he is the reason you're here. And because of our friendship that you're here... I dunno. I don't know how it will all work out, but sometimes you have to forgive to be forgiven... You'll know it when the time comes for that stuff; no one can tell you."

When you go into her house, you are punched in the face with the smell of things green and it's incredibly obvious she loves plants with ferns, trees and various other foliage lining the walls and windows. She takes care of every single one of them by herself. One of her granddaughters told me she even tried growing Marijuana although it wasn't for what you might think. Her reasoning was because she thought the flowers looked pretty. One day a fellow officer saw these and said something to her along the lines of "Don't you know these are illegal?" Her response was a simple "What are you going to do, arrest me?" Valid question. Who is going to arrest a 90-year-old woman? No one that's who. "Ain't no one the boss of me."

Fay Key is woman of wisdom, a woman of love with positivity infectious and infinite. "I just know so much junk and I love to get it out." It's not junk and good luck, I can tell you try. Thank-you for being there and doing the good thing. Good luck on your plans to visit the Grand Canyon with Ken in the afterlife. He knows his way around those parts and I'm positive you'll have a good time.

*Dad's Letter*
*No Date*
*Dear Mrs. Key*

*I love getting your letters. I read them through right when I get them and read them again later to make sure I caught everything you were really saying in them.*

*I think God puts a variety of people in our lives so we can learn from and share things with each one of them. I didn't always enjoy hearing my dads stories when he told them but now I realize the value of them and my brothers and sister still talk about some of them even though our dad died twenty-five years ago now. I remember some of his stories about growing up during the depression too and I know that had an effect on me even if they were just from stories my dad told. Much like yours.*

*I remember when I was in first grade my mom and dad didn't have a lot of extra money at the time either. They chose to send all four of us kids to Christian School and had to struggle to pay the bills. At the beginning of the school year my class each got a slip of paper to take home so our parents could order white milk for $1.50 or chocolate milk for $1.75. I didn't give the slip to my mom because I didn't think we could afford it. Two days went by at school and I sat there with no milk while all the other kids got their milk after the morning recess. My teacher must have asked my mom about it because my mom asked me about why I didn't give her the milk order for me. When I told her I didn't think we could afford it she lovingly laughed and said they could pay for the milk for the semester. Since the white milk was cheaper, I asked for the white milk.*

*One day during that semester I tried the chocolate milk of one of the other kids. It was so good that I could not wait until the second semester so I could order chocolate milk even if it was 25¢ more. That second semester I savored every drop of my chocolate milk and I have thought of my first grade year every time I've had chocolate milk ever since. It's amazing how God gives us little memories like that so we can enjoy things for the rest of our lives.*

*One story I remember from my dad is a story he only told once that I recall but a story that had a big impact on my life. It's not a heroic or exciting story by far but it is very low key. My dad was drafted during the Korean War in 1951. Soon after Basic Training he and a friend drove home from Ft. Jackson, North Carolina during a three day pass. Dad had to see his girlfriend- who in turn became his wife and my mom. While they were driving back his friend fell asleep and they got into a bad accident. My dad spent almost the next eighteen months in an army hospital. His right leg femur was severally broken so he was in traction for a long time. There was an older WWII vet that was a sergeant who worked as an orderly on my dad's floor. (I write all this to get to the main story.)*

*All the patients would get a paper carton of milk or juice on their food tray. My dad said that old sergeant scolded him or someone else close by him for not folding up the empty carton and crushing it flat. He said just because they were laid up in the hospital they were still soldiers and could still help the war effort. If they didn't flatten the carton, and if nobody did, the cartons would take up twice as much space in the garbage and someone would have to make two trips to the dump instead of one. My dad said he thought it was kind of silly at first and it made him a little angry. After a while he realized the sergeant's motive was more to keep the bed ridden men from feeling sorry for themselves. Making them do something was meant to keep them contributing in any way they could. To this day I always flatten my drink carton whenever I have one.*

*You asked how my kids are doing. My brother says they are doing well. My daughter, Bre, is busy in school and with friends. She is planning on going south for spring break with some friends and their parents. Then after graduating high school she will be off to Calvin College in the fall. She is such a blessing to everyone she meets. God's love just shows through in everything she does. I couldn't imagine a young lady with a more God filled life.*

*My son Chris is a quiet sixteen year old young man but he doesn't miss anything and socializes a lot with a good group of friends. He's very smart and gets all A's even in advanced classes. He has wanted to be a doctor for the last ten years and is working hard for it. He is already looking for good Pre-medical school colleges to attend two years from now. I know that God is a big part of his life by the choices he has been making. He started taking responsibility for his spiritual life a while back ands started going to a different church with some good friends. What more could I want? So I just pray that they continue to grow in their walk with God.*

*I hope your family is doing well. It must keep you busy keeping track of them all. It sounds like you are still busy with your church too. You will have to live to be 100 in order to do all the things you want to do. Your writing class sounds like something I should have done years ago. I wish I was a better writer now but there is always time to improve.*

*Thank you for staying in touch.*
*Your Brother in Christ,*
*Ken*


*Dad's Letter*
*Wednesday March 19, 2008*
*Dear Friend, Fay Key,*

*Well not much has changed in my life. I have a lot of time to think and you got me started reminiscing about all the fond memories of my childhood because of what you wrote in your last letter. I have thought of memories during this last week that I have not thought of in a long time. It helps to think of a context or place and it brings up old memories.*

*I have always loved spring time most of all. Easter seemed to mean a little more to me than even Christmas because it didn't have all the commercialism with it. Easter* was just Easter, without all the distractions of presents. Soon afterward came the end of the school year. That meant all the special events like class trips, Memorial Day, Tulip Time and of course the last day of school. That was always bittersweet since we lived way out in the country and I would not see most of my friends all summer long. I had figured out that I lived farther away from school than anyone else. It just meant that during the summer you did things with relatives or neighborhood kids.

One summer after first and second grade, my mom came home from grocery shopping with a kite! My brother, four years older, put it together right away and took it outside. It happened to be a perfect day for kite flying right then and for the next few days. The neighbor boys had gotten a kite too so for the next few days we sat in the wheat field next to our farm and watched our kite fly. It took a little while to fly it well because an old fashioned tail had to be added on to the bottom of it to make it fly better. I can still picture it flying because it had a skull and cross bones on it like a pirate's flag. I had the feeling like we were on top of the world. Of course we almost were. Our farm house was on the second highest place in the county of Ottawa my dad said but I'm not 100% sure on that. I do know that despite being 1 3/4 miles east of Drenthe we could see the outline of the dunes on Lake Michigan and the smoke stack of the Consumers Power Plant at Port Sheldon- eighteen miles away as the crow flies. It seems like we laid in that wheat field for hours watching the two kites lazy days of summer. They don't get any better. Of course summer didn't really start until June 20 but that didn't matter to us.

Summer break also meant that we could explore all the woods around the farm and neighboring farms. Years before people used to dump all their trash off in the woods *somewhere. We would find those and spend hours looking through it all, finding all kinds of treasure. Or, we would just look for things to smash. Best of all were glass bottles with old stuff still in them. To break it open and see what it smelled like was great fun. It really is amazing that we all lived through it.*

*I'm just laughing to myself about other memories I have about the end of the school year. I was about five or six when I figured out that there was no vacation from church. After the last day of school when the next Sunday came I asked my mom why we had to go to church. "Don't we get a vacation from church?" I asked. I remember her explaining that it was a blessing to be able to go every week. We of course went morning and evening every Sunday. Now I appreciate that my parents had that mind set and made going to church a priority.*

*I like it when you share tales from your childhood and I like to share my tales with someone that can understand. I think that growing up in a rural area or community has so many advantages. There is something to be said, or a lot of truth to the statement that it is the responsibility of the entire community the bring up its youth. When I was young I knew all the older people in Drenthe Church and I knew where they lived. You just don't get that these days any more in churches. At least not in mine. There are some things that are better now but unfortunately it seems that when things change we lose some good things to get other good things. Wouldn't it be great to get rid of only the bad and take on only the good.*

*I've been keeping this letter for a few days and just adding to it when I have a chance. It's Easter today! What a great day this is. I can't image what life would be like without Easter and knowing that Jesus rose from the dead for me and everyone else. All the sins I've done are forgiven because I've asked God for forgiveness. That makes me just sit here and think about how wonderful God is.*

*This morning I had a visit from an old friend of mine. He has been blessed by God after having been through some very difficult times in life himself and can really relate to me with my situation. Not all of my friends are able to relate and understand his point. Some have even written to say they doubt my salvation. It is hard to hear but it does make me step back and examine myself again. Plus, in a way I'm glad they have not had some difficult times in their lives. If they need a trial to make themselves see clearly, it will be up to God. I try to think, just like you wrote in your first letter, about being nobodies judge. I find that if I am getting down in the dumps here it is because I am thinking about what other people are thinking of me. I need to remember to focus on how I am with God. So, whenever I get a discouraging letter I remember what you wrote. I also try to remember that they are speaking in love the best way they know how.*

*Well I'll get this out before it gets too long. Thanks for staying in touch. I enjoy getting your letters and being one of the several people you write to.*

*Your friend,*
*Ken*


*Dad's Letter*
*Tuesday Feb 26, 2008*
*Dear Ms. Key,*

*I have been thinking a lot about you and the letters you have from your brother that fought in the Pacific during WWII. I just read two novels that started out with men who were fighting the Japanese in the jungles during* the war. Even though the books are novels, a lot of the historical setting is factual and based on real events. Reading about those events and the incredible acts of bravery by so many men and women makes me kind of envious of your generation- The Greatest Generation.

On the other hand I think my generation may be more fortunate than yours. We did not have to endure WWII but we did get to reap the benefits of those that lived before us. My dad was in the Army during the Korean War but he taught me to appreciate all the history and stories from WWII.

I have a lot of time to reflect on several things and remember different people I have been blessed to have met. You are surely one of them. Having read your books it seems like I know you very well, better than I would know most people I would only talk with from time to time. For that I am thankful. From you I learned, and I'm still learning, that it is OK to share your weaknesses. I hope that if I can share my weaknesses that God can still use me in some way. I know I'll never write a book but I know that we were all put here to glorify God so even though I failed in some ways I hope to still do some now.

I hope you are well and still making it outdoors some time in spite of this terrible winter it sounds like you are having. If I were you I would stay in the house from December to April. However, with you being the way you are I would think that staying indoors that much would be difficult. Just don't go skiing or sledding down any big hills.

Thank you again for the letters and also for the prayers for Bre, Chris and me. Thank you for the memories of our visits and for the wisdom you shared during those times. Now if I know you, you will wonder what kind of wisdom you gave me. Well you were always willing to share some of God's truths with me and there is no greater

*wisdom than that.*
   *Your friend Ken*

# Chapter 7: The Crux Move

*Dad's Letter*
*October 13, 2008*
*Dear Toph,*
*I've just been thinking about it being your junior year and realized this is the first time you're not in the same school as Bre. She may have been in a different building as you but she was always around in person or by presence. Fortunately Bre had a good presence and she was easy to follow. More importantly you made your own way and reputation that was always outstanding. You may have followed Bre but you never depended on her or remained in her shadow.*

*I guess I've been thinking about this because your sister is turning nineteen today. You are seventeen and two weeks as of today and it makes me think about how time has flown. For almost twenty years God has blessed this world with the two of you. I cannot imagine any son being more of a blessing to those around him than you are. Each time I think of the time that you were voted, "Most Christ-like" by your class, I think that wherever you are, people will think the same thing of you. That's why I am confident that you did something to make your sister's birthday a special day for her. She may be off at Calvin but I'm sure that you still mean the world to her. In fact, I'd be surprised if she doesn't try talking you into going to Calvin after a while. Not that she ever needed to keep you under her wing or anything, but I suspect that she would love to see you have the same fun that she is having her freshman year.*

*October 30, 2008*

*I went to my Wednesday night Bible study last night and remember something from it I would like to share with you. We were talking about family relationships and a statement was said that stuck with me and I think makes a lot of sense. The study leader said, "Wounded hearts wound hearts." Whenever you read this, please think about that statement and take it to heart. It's easy to forget that others have been wounded which effects our relationship with them. It's also easy to deny that we have been wounded and not think about how that effects the way we treat others. I have been wounded and without realizing it I can easily wound others without thinking about it. I know I have wounded you and if you don't realize that, you may continue that cycle and wound others. I could go on and on with memories of how I may have wounded you. Perhaps I should do that some day but now I just want to say how very much I always loved you and felt blessed to have you as a son.*

*Another thing or side to remember about, "Wounded hearts wound hearts" is that when others wound you, that is a reaction to their having been wounded in the past. You or I may not intentionally wound someone because of what they are doing or did, but because of what someone else did to us. This is all a result of sin and what happens because of it, that gets passed down from generation to generation, from relationship to relationship, or even from best friend to best friend. Nobody can be perfect but I know that with God's help, people can break that cycle. I pray that God helps you break anything bad that I may have passed on to you. I was never perfect so I know there are some ways I've wounded both you and Bre but God can help you overcome even that. When I think of ways that I have wounded you it may be totally different than the ways that you think I've wounded you. Someday we will be able to talk about that.*

*We will also be able to talk about how God did, is, and will help each of us get past and heal from our wound. I know God has helped you cope in the past because I've always been able to see Jesus working in and through you. Nobody can be as much of a blessing to others like you have been unless they have Jesus in their heart like you have.*

*I love you bud. I hope someday you can realize that and know that. Bre and you have been and are an amazing gift to me from God. I've tried to keep the two of you first but sometimes I failed at that. Please forgive me for my failures and look to any blessing that I tried to pass on to you. Keep that faith.*

*"Faith is not to be confused with determination optimism, or imagination. Actually it is simply believing. It is knowing there is an ocean because you have seen a brook; a mountain because you have seen a hill; God because you have seen a human."*

*Dad*


*Mom's Journal*
*No Date*
*I am often in a place of struggle, somewhere between a rock and a hard place. No choice seems good or easy or maybe even tolerable. Talking it out helps, but audiences and advisors seem few.*

*Then there's Tipper. I call her my Jesus Kitty. As I peer into her eyes, the greens and browns around her almond shaped pupils somehow calm my mind in a way that only Jesus could. Her nudge, her purr remind me that she's there and that she loves me cuz I'm special. When I am trying to focus on something like a newspaper or book, she invariably plants herself in such a way that I must refocus what I'm doing, being reminded that she is far more important than anything else on my mind or in her way. On the nights when my mind is deeply troubled, she just knows; and like Jesus she wraps herself around my troubled head and purrs because she loves me.*

Dad's Letter
Thursday
May 19, 2010
Dear Toph,
    *You are nineteen years old and that's so exciting for me to think about. After an exciting summer in the Tetons, I'll bet you have caught the bug for wanting to take some other adventures in the future. The great thing is that you can make a big adventure out of lots of different things and a lot of places. Heck, working at the Brewery could be it's own adventure.*
    *This letter comes with a lot of prayers Toph. Every morning I pray for you that God may bless you and keep you. It certainly sounds like God is blessing you and keeping you. Everyone says you are so self-assured and happy. I love to hear that. I imagine you do such a great job at the Brewery and several people have said you do very well with video and film. It sounds like you have found something you really enjoy and are good at at the same time. Go for it!*
    *I am sure you feel very loved by Keith, Jan and the rest of the family. Even though they already love you very much I still ask Keith to give you my love along with theirs most every time I talk with him. Since you were old enough to understand I would ask you if you knew that I loved you. You would say that you knew that. I hope you still know that now. Please try and remember that, as well as the fact that God loves you too.*

*Everyday I am reminded that God loves me too. The biggest way is when I hear how well you and Bre are doing. One of the biggest ways God has blessed me here is by people who let me know what a wonderful young man you have turned out to be. I cannot think of much more that I would want for you. May God make you like Ephrain and Manasseh.*
*Love Dad*


"Wounded hearts wound hearts." While this is true and can inspire one to empathy, it is not a good place to stop thinking. Perhaps we have all been wounded and some people need some help healing, but dwelling on peoples' wounds can lead to pity which is no substitution for compassion. What happens to a fractured bone or tree branch when it heals? It becomes stronger than before. If you chose to see yourself as wounded, that is what you will be. If you chose to see yourself as a healed or healing person, that is who can and will become. Victimhood is a trap that is easy to fall into. Once we see ourselves as a victim of circumstance, we dissolve responsibility for our own actions and give that responsibility to our circumstance instead. Happiness can exist with suffering in all phenomena.

From *The New Jim Crow* by Michelle Alexander:

"None of this is to suggest that those who break the law bear no responsibility for their conduct or exist merely as 'products of their environment.' To deny the individual agency of those caught up in the system - their capacity to overcome seemingly impossible odds - would be to deny an essential element of their humanity. We, as human beings, are not simply organisms or animals responding to stimuli. We have a higher self, a capacity for transcendence."

Hatred and anger are very easy things to let linger. Anger is a dangerous fuel that can drive you forward while simultaneously holding you back. It feels good. It's an emotional and action-less revenge, a two headed viper: while you are stomping on one head, the other is biting you in the heal. You are convinced your anger is somehow making things better and discover too many ways to justify it. Of course, I was pretty pissed when dad killed mom and many times I told myself I was never going to see him again; that he deserved to rot where he stands. Obviously that is no longer true, otherwise I wouldn't be writing this sentence. Time heals all wounds and many things happened in order for me to relinquish my anger towards my own father. I'm not perfect, some days I have to try harder than others, but it only gets easier and it's only gotten better. Eventually I learned these kind of emotions, no matter how compartmentalized you think they are, bleed into all aspects of life and affect even the littlest of decisions.

Emotional repression is real. For a long time, I tried to convince myself I could get past all the shit that happened or it didn't affect me. Boy was I wrong. There were many times in many classes where something would come up, either a project or a conversation, in which I would have something to contribute based on my dreadful experiences. Instead of using the things I learned, I refused to let it come out and talk about it and was either left in silence or some bullshit explanation I didn't actually believe in and made up to avoid the topic. I told myself I didn't want to stick out or metaphorically profit and take advantage of my situation. Also, I didn't like the attention; I didn't want my own pity party. I am a proud and stoic Dutchman after all. Although there were times when I would write about my history and I would hand it in thinking, "This is such heavy shit, there's no way I'm not getting an A. Even if everything besides the sad stuff is mediocre." It worked every time. But here I am spending day after day dwelling, writing page after page and maybe I'll make a literal profit out of this book. We are all wounded people and we all show it different ways, whether it be writing a book or yelling at the manager in Walgreens on the corner of the block.

One thing that began this whole thought process was something one of my high school friends said. He said, "Anger only effects the beholder," so unless you are going to do something about it, you end up just sitting in the sediment and stew of your own negative emotions. And there I was bumming around high school, thinking the world owed me something. It doesn't- I have to take it. I let the wisdom of that quote sink in and began to apply it to every emotion. Unless you are going to do something to fix it, emotion can sit in a state of stagnancy and ruin a person. Seek help; either from within or without, it doesn't matter as long as you are trying. Meditate or see a therapist. Do something about it. Preferably not drugs as they are more like just throwing a newspaper over a puddle of piss your puppy left you on the floor. I tried the whole SSRI thing and after a while it felt more like a fog had fallen over my face and figured if I was going to medicate, I might as well go back to smoking weed because at least that comes with a bit of fun. Although it helped by dissolving certain aspects of my personality, it didn't change what I felt about what happened or help in the pursuit of self betterment. Your brain is a muscle and all it needs is a little training.

That friend's phrase has stuck with me to this day, but a few other things helped along the way. Finding your sense of spirituality helps the most. Pick something that makes you feel like a better person, puts you on a positive path and commit. You don't always have to express it or preach it like a vegan Crossfitter- you just have to know it for yourself. There are as many types of spirituality as there are people in this world. I know what mine is, you never will and I suggest you find your own.

    Film has always been my favorite medium and with television climbing up the production value latter, they have both had a major impact on me. Never underestimate the lessons you can learn from art; my favorite happens to be that of visual story telling, whether it be film or television. Watching the show *Dexter* was another major turning point for me. It may sound odd, I know it does to me, but watching a show about a serial killer made me like my dad a little bit more. The series is about a serial killer who went through traumatic experiences, feels these "dark urges" to kill, but redirects those urges to only kill bad guys. In a nonliteral way, I fell in love with a serial killer and thought, "If this guy was real, I'd still empathize with him. He went through some shit and is making the best out of a murderous situation." Then I started thinking about my dad. He is real and he is just a person. I know he went through some shit- I was there. Why haven't I empathized with him?

    There have been a couple other shows flooding my brain with positive thinking. Two of them being *Avatar: The Last Airbender* and *Legend of Korra*. But the point of this paragraph comes from *Legend of Korra*. It is about a girl whose name is- you guessed it- Korra. She goes through a traumatic experience of being poisoned and almost murdered. After a long recovery of repression and self-delusion she finally realizes, while facing the final boss, she has to win with empathy, not violence. Before her attempted murder, she was overconfident and egotistical, but became depressed and physically unable to do what she used to love- fight. She ends up winning the war through empathetical conversation and vocally realizes she had to go through all the terrible things in order to become compassionate towards other people. I believe the same thing. Not just because I have to in order to feel better, but because it is what I choose.

Violence is hardly ever the final answer nor can I commit to saying my life would be better without it. How could anyone possibly know? He said he wanted a normal family for me and this was the only way to make it possible. People have asked him why he didn't just kill John Doe. It's because John Doe was a simple spoke in my mom's wagon wheel of infatuation. Ken said he thought she would just fall in love with someone else and keep that train running. Knowing about her past now, this is easy for me to understand, but death is not the answer and at some point you have to be okay with not being loved by someone. I wish I could go back and have the wherewithal to tell my dad, "She doesn't love you anymore. Just give up. It's okay, these things happen. I still love you." Poor bastard kept trying to force something that wasn't there. I don't know if he was blinded by the traditional Christian commitment of marriage, an ego or self image, wanting to keep it together for my sister and I, or still had that much love for her. I guess it can be all of them.

What about hope for a second chance, or in my mother's case a sixth chance? What if she could change? Despite evidence and patterns depicting otherwise, I refuse to believe she was hopeless. We tried many things to help her, but nothing worked, which left only one option in the mind of my father. We may never know what would have happened to her if she wasn't killed, but we know the reality of now and we have to deal with it. I am happy with the reality that's been given, warts and all. "What if" is a koan that can never be answered.

Within my collegiate attempts, there came Freshman Seminar, a required class in college that everyone hated but me. We had a project, and since it was art school, I had free reign over the idea and how to present it. The project was "Do art with a point." This is where I began to read the letters my father wrote; the letters that had been piling up for years. Fortunately they were all kept in a box, awaiting my return. My idea for the project was to write a journal from my father's perspective leading up to and following the murder. I changed some details, but it was entirely based off of the letters he wrote. This project made me incredibly uncomfortable but it felt right and timely so I pursued it. Within this, I explored what could have been going on in his head and realized this is something, this is someone I can empathize with, despite the horrible tragedy. It was at this point, I decided it was okay for him to write me directly. Eventually this led to my first visit and an ongoing relationship.

Empathy is being able to understand someone, or in other words, put yourself in their shoes. Despite my long term hatred for my father, I found my years of youth being incredibly similar to his. Our main similarity being a general lust for adventure and novelty. He worked in a few camps out in Colorado and California when he was my age and always loved to travel. Since I am writing this sentence in a garden in Myanmar, staring down a wooden elephant and a literal water buffalo, I can't help but feel that connection.

About two weeks out of high school I moved out west for the summer. I was given an awesome opportunity to work in Grand Teton National Park at Colter Bay Campground. The application was submitted in the January before the summer and my friend liked the idea so decided to apply with me. If he hadn't done that, I might not have got the job because he is a sociable person with a silver tongue and made the call to the application department. After a schmooze, the manager showed his appreciation by pulling both our applications to the top. The deal was sealed, a plane did we yield off to the land of mountains and fields. I could say that was the best summer of my life to make it sound more amazing, but then I'd feel bad for the other summers which I make awesome every time. People from all over the world, from every wake of life worked there in hopes to get a glimpse of the mild west. My muslim friend and I would talk religion over Turkish Silvers between bathroom cleanings. A devout Mormon claimed me to be his primordial friend, meaning we were friends in Heaven before we were vaginally expelled into the material world. Almost got attacked by a bear while sightseeing with a one-legged Vietnam veteran, although I stayed calm because I knew I'd be able to outrun at least one person. Morning hikes and lunch time bikes; blistered toes up mountainous foes; tea drinking dopes with a pipe to smoke. Good times were, are, and will be.

    Ken calls this part of the book the Crux Move. In mountain climbing, the Crux Move is the most difficult position and determines whether or not you will make it the rest of the way up. Confidently, ten years after the murder, I can say I will make it to the top in hopes that there will only be further mountains to climb. My dad also said I was being too modest about my transformation and should expand on that. The more I thought about it, the more I realized I really have nothing more to say. What changed me was the letters he wrote and instead of telling you how that affected me positively as an individual, I want to show you the letters in hopes that you won't compare yourself to me but find your own truths within them. There is not one single move that has defined this climb but a series of situations and decisions. It took reading through hundreds of letters to me, to Keith and Jan, to Fay Key that transformed him from what I thought was a monster into a human.

*Dad's Letter*
*December 25, 2008*
*Dear Keith,*
 *Man, it was so good to see you this last Saturday. It was good to see [Friend] too. It made my day and my whole week because it was so good to hear what is going on with everyone but also to share what is going on with me to the both of you.*
 *I'll admit that it has been easy to avoid facing the holidays or think about them at all. I've not written any letters out for the last week and a half because it's easier not to think about it all that way. On the other hand, this has been one of the best Christmases ever for me because I don't have all the business that goes along with it out in the world. When all else is stripped away and it's just me with God, I can honestly say that this is one of the more peaceful Christmases I've had. This morning, Christmas morning, after my prayers for family and friends, I reread all the Christmas cards I got from everyone. It does no good to dwell on memories or thing about "What if?" So I haven't been doing that. I trust that Bre and Toph are having a good Christmas and that Lori is having the best one of all.*
 *I got a package from [Church] this last Tuesday with thirty some cards in it. There were a lot of nice notes of encouragement with the cards. That meant very much to me. Could you get a "Thank you" to church for me please? Oh, never mind. I've been writing a couple from church so I'll ask them to pass on a Thank-You.*
 *It seems that some people may be feeling a little sorry*

*for me in this first holiday season but I'm really very good about everything. I've been making some good friends by talking with some of them and just listening to what they are going through or struggling with. Some guys just really need to talk about what it's like for them.*

*For a prayer request, if anyone asks, just let them know to thank God that [Prison Friend] is in my life here as a fellow Christian that encourages me. Also that God continues to work in [Other Prison Friend] because he is really struggling through this season. He misses his family like everyone but he knows that he may never be able to get together with them again. Sometimes I spend time with [Prison Friend] so that I can be a better help to [Other Prison Friend] and some other guys.*

*You know it never dawned on me that people might think that [My Lover] had a hand in putting me up to murdering Lori. When [Friend] said that, I was surprised that people thought of that and I never considered that people might think that. I don't think [My Lover] thought of that either so I think that will explain some things to her when I tell her about that. The ironic thing is that she unknowingly was one of the larger influences to not go through with it. She was talking the greatest sense in how to deal with Lori than most.*

*I know she hasn't contacted you because she doesn't want to make it difficult for you at all. Not to mention that she is very busy all the time. She starts a seven week class in January. If she passes that she has one more class to go to and she will be done.*

*Well I have to get this out. Take care and have a happy New Year.*

*Love*
*Brother Ken*

*Dad's Letter*
*February 9, 2012*
*Dear Toph,*
    I just talked on the phone to Keith a few days ago and he said it would be alright for me to write you directly. That is no small thing to me. That's an understatement really. It's a huge thing to be able to write you directly. Before I always felt I was writing you and a bunch of other people too. I hope you realize that some people thought I should wait a while and leave it up to you to ask about communicating with you instead of me writing to you right away. I am thrilled to write you.
    First let me say I am sorry for any and every way I have wronged you or made things difficult for you. Some of those wrongs are obvious but I'm sure there are other wrongs I have not thought of. You can always feel free to tell me about those things or ask me about anything you wonder about.
    Geez! I just remembered now that I am writing to a writer. Mom and Ade tell me you are studying Journalism. That's great! But for me, I've always been self conscious about my writing, penmanship, grammar, and spelling. Now here I am writing to my son who is a writer and no doubt very good at it, making me think twice about everything I write. Thankfully I have a Webster's Dikshonairy for my spelling.
    It felt funny getting used to writing [my fourth grade teacher]. She has sent me several cards and letters so I responded to her a few times. At first it was weird but I remember her as always being so nice and she was my favorite teacher- way back in 1972. For some reason she remembered me all those years since then. But that isn't as bad as when I write old [Friend] from [Church].

*Remember him? He was the church librarian with his wife. He has been a book editor for in Grand Rapids for over fifty years. Oh well, he is understanding and will cut me some slack. I haven't gotten any letters back marked up with a red marker yet.*

*Mom and Ade told me when they were visiting that you were focusing on a specific kind of journalism and doing some writing. I'm sure you will do really well with that. You will do well with whatever you choose to do. You've always been blessed with doing well with whatever you want. If you would ever feel comfortable sending me something you have written, I would love to read it. Yes, I still brag about you and Bre as much as I can around here. My favorite picture I have to show off you and Bre is the one of you and Bre on the day Bre moved in to her Calvin dorm. You are both sitting on the floor in front of the book case eating Snyder pretzels with big smiles on your faces. That was three and a half years ago already.*

*Later: Wow! I just got back from my Calvin Seminary class I'm taking here. This class is called "Forgiveness and Reconciliation." We are reading a book about he South African Apartheid and how they got rid of some of the hurt from all the years of racism from the whites who ruled. They finally got rid of all the Apartheid law about the year you were born. It's quite a story and something I can learn from.*

*Remember that I pray for you everyday either first thing in the morning and as I go to sleep at night. Not to mention several times during each day. It certainly seems that God is answering my prayers for you because from everything I hear about you, you are doing fantastic. Fantastic in school, life and the choices you are making. I'm sure it is not easy but keep it up.*

*I want to reiterate to you that you can ask me about*

*anything you want and I'll do my best to answer it. I understand it may not be easy for you or for me but ask what ever you want to.*

# Chapter 8: Behind Bars

*Dad's Letter*
*December 28, 2011*
*Dear Bre and Toph,*
    *I just finished reading the first letter of John. [Our friend] suggested in a letter that I read that book from time to time. They are pretty smart about such things so I take her up on her advice and read it a few times a year. I make the same suggestion to other people too and most respond favorably.*
    *This card comes with many hopes and prayers for the both of you. I know that both of you are doing well and facing the joys and challenges with the adventurous spirits each of you have. For me, looking back at the years you are in now, life was such a swirl of constant change going from one exciting challenge to another. I pray that God allows both of you keep to keep growing as people in his world.*
    *The way I came about this Hallmark card in prison is no small miracle. It's not much of an exaggeration to say that my once possible, would be persecutor who has become my friend and protector gave it to me to send to you. I met Newby (who goes by "Packman") on February 26, 2011, a few days after I transferred to Ionia. We started working in the kitchen for Food Service on the same day. He is a big mean looking black guy from the streets of Kalamazoo. He had a bad attitude about my distance from him as he moved into a position of washing pots and pans and I became a lead cook. A few months ago he needed help so I helped him out washing. He liked my work so I kept helping him for a few days. Eventually he told me what he was in prison for. He had killed two guys after they had done a drive by on his house and shot to death his five-*

*year-old son. His name was Derek and at five years old he "looked just like me," Packman said. This tough hard ass who got the name "Packman" by "squeezing out" other drug dealers on the streets melted as he told me about his son. Since then he has been my friend and he is a good "big" friend to have.*

*A few days later when Packman and I were working, someone else asked me if I had really been a cop. When I was honest and told him I had been a cop for fourteen years, Packman didn't believe me at first. He wanted me to prove it but when I told him I didn't care if he believed me or not then he believed me. We still remain friends even though we don't work together. Of course I have told Packman all about the two of you as you were growing up. He knows how proud I am of the two of you. A few days ago he came up to me wanting to give me this card so I could send it to you. I appreciate that act of kindness and the fact that he thought of you both. He said, "Kenny, you got to send this card to your kids!"*

*Your dad is out of shape and getting fatter. I cook for the third shift officers so I get to eat as much as I want of what is there. That means I do too little and eat too much.*

*A couple friends here and I got Calvin Theological Seminary to start giving some classes here in the prison. Fourteen of us just finished a class- "Living and Dying with Christ." It was a lot of reading and some writing each week but everyone did it. Next semester the class is called, "Forgiveness and Reconciliation." Please pray that I am able to work through some things in that class. All fourteen of us in the class hope to be a good influence on the 1,200 other guys around us. In some ways this is a pretty dark place but we try to let our lights shine.*

*My prayer for the both of you is that you can let your lights shine in your worlds also. I'm sure you both give joy to your worlds and the people around you just like you always did to me. I'm thinking of the squeals of laughter the two of you would make as I drove to Colorado and the boredom of the long drive got to you. Once the long road trip got monotonous you would get silly and that would lead to squeals of laughter coming from the back of the van. I sometimes just shook my head with a smirk on my face as I drove along. Keith and I used to do the same thing. Imagine that!*

    *I don't know what I can write or do to encourage you more. If I could I would but please know that I pray for you often each day.*

    *Love Dad*

*Dad's Letter*
*Excerpt from February 9, 2012*

    *On a personal note, my feet hurt. I walked a couple of miles today with my friend. We walked on the big loop path during yard time. He is quite a talker so I like to talk about where he is from. He is a twenty-three year old black guy from Manistee and I'm one of the only guys that knows anything about where he is from. We started hanging out and going to church together because, as he says or tells me, I'm the only guy that smiles almost as much as he does. He's a nice kid but very impulsive so that gets him in trouble. One reason he hangs out with me is to keep him out of trouble but honestly, I don't feel I'm much of a role model. Better than most around here I guess. He calls me "Uncle Ken."*

    *I'll keep this short. Sometimes I ramble on and on because people genuinely want to know about what this life is like for me. They ask, I tell them.*

    *I hope you had a good week. I think of you and Bre often and pray for you always.*

*Love,*
*Dad*


After five long years of anger and confusion, searching and discovery, I was ready to confront my dad. I had written a whole bunch of juicy questions I was going to ask him- about my mom, about why he killed her and how he did it and what was going through his head. It wasn't that I wanted to drill him with these questions because I wanted to make him feel bad or anything. I knew what I wanted and that was answers.

Silence was all there was on the car ride out, about a two hour drive. The first time was just Keith and I. He said this is what every drive up is like with prison visit virgins. I was nervous about everything: getting into the prison, seeing other convicts, seeing my dad for the first time in five years, if I was going to be able to get those questions out of my mouth while looking the man in the face. Sure I was nervous as hell, but I knew this was the time and it needed to be done, which gave me some sort of existential calm. When I finally made the decision, there were no second thoughts.

Seconds before entering the visiting room, my heart and head began to pound like an African bongo. It was at that point I realized I had no idea what to expect. Usually I go through various scenarios in my head but this time it was still, which comforted me because it felt right- like I both needed and wanted to be there. Plus Keith said beforehand I was in complete control; I could leave whenever I wanted- it was my afternoon. He'll always be there.

We went through the check-in, where union correction officers apathetically took our information and gave us a number to wait. We handed in our identification, sat down and after they took our belongings, they called my dad from whatever activity he was doing. Could have been work, could have been yard time, could have been fighting off a bull queer. We had to pass through two sets of steel bar doors and in the middle was a metal detector and a frisking station. As the doors slowly clanked open, the lady knocked on the window and told me I couldn't enter with a hooded sweatshirt. *Could have told me this when we checked in, but whatever.* It did bum me out a little because it was a sweatshirt I had screen printed and wanted to show him but I proceeded to strip anyway. But then the shirt I had underneath had a few small holes, so that was a no-go as well. *Okay then.* A moment of panic until Keith said we could go into town and pick up a shirt, so we hastily left the building. On the way out he realized he was wearing two shirts so he gave me one and I threw it on. It was large so I looked like a child but at least we were able to get in. Now I bring two sets of clothes every time, just in case.

The gentleman who frisked us was really nice. He made small talk with us, joked, and laughed but I can't remember any of it because I wasn't paying attention and just nodded and smiled. We took everything out of our pockets, took off our jewelry and glasses then proceeded through a metal detector where they checked everything: our shoes, our socks, even our mouths, but not our butt holes thankfully. I had a ponytail at the time, which they didn't check, and I thought about all the shivs and drugs I could have hidden. *Next time.* It was quick and painless but I bet if we had someone less friendly feeling us up, it wouldn't have gone so smoothly. So thank-you Ionia Corrections Officer, you made that part easy on me. We displayed our hands under the black light to reveal the magic ink they marked us with and went into the visiting room. *This is happening.*

Ken was right around the corner sitting, waiting, wishing. Although he had shoes on and was without an acoustic guitar. They made the inmates sit down, away from the door while they waited so they wouldn't attempt to bolt through the steel cage. There he sat with a loosely fitted green polo shirt, navy jeans and black orthopedic shoes. He had aged in five years, go figure and he wasn't kidding in his letter: he gained some weight and whatever hair he had left was turning gray. There was a smile on his face and a few visibly restrained tears.

My first reaction was surprise because I didn't expect him to be so calm and jovial. Prison was treating him well, apparently. Every single smile was ear to ear and full fledged; it's like he was happy to see me or something. For a while I couldn't pinpoint what this reminded me of but a few hours into the meeting it dawned on me: he reminded me of the Dalai Llama and all the videos I had seen of his contagious smiles and laughter. The calmness he had was infectious and I found my soul instantly smoothed and glazed with contentedness for being right then and there. This was not what I expected at all.

I was speechless at first and had no idea what to say based on what was in front of me. Luckily he had some presence of mind and started asking me about what I had been doing with my life in the past five years. The first couple hours was a bunch of life talk and reminiscing about camping and all the trips we had taken. I hadn't expected to smile and laugh so much, but within two minutes we were laughing together like nothing ever happened or maybe that's what we were trying to convince ourselves. I brought up this book, the one you're reading. Keith had told him about it with my permission, so naturally he was incredibly curious. At one point he asked me the title. It was weird for me to say out loud for some reason, but I told him the working title, which has since changed, was "How I Came to Love the Man Who Murdered My Mother." His head flew back in surprise and he started weeping. "Oooooh bud...."

The questions I came with were not forgotten and eventually we got to the more heavy topics. But it really didn't change anything and it was all things I already found out through my research. He had already told people about all this and I found out through them. I don't know what I expected to learn, but I still needed to hear it come from his mouth, regardless of anything coming to light. We talked about the night him, Keith and another friend confronted my mom in the kitchen to no avail. He kept getting sidetracked by other details and a little hesitant about some. Keith reminded him a few times that I was ready to hear everything and to hold nothing back- warts and all.

My father was a completely different man than I had known him to be, granted I didn't have too many great memories of him. He went to Iraq when I was in seventh grade and when he got back the divorce bullshit started so he was frequently stressed out and warped because of it. The only positive memories I had of him were from before middle school and I was so young, those memories were becoming faded. This would make it almost ten years since I'd seen the "real" him.

The conversation was a cocktail mixture of serious and fun things. I asked him a few questions about what life was like for the incarcerated version of him. He was unbelievable content with where he was and said he knew what he did was wrong and was where he deserved to be. Regret isn't the right word for it though; that's called acceptance and he was incredibly okay with his situation and at peace with himself. He had even gotten some education when he was there and which was obvious based on his vocabulary and conversation skills. Even in his letters, I could tell because he was using words like "assuage" and he even corrected me on a couple things and that's never happened.

    We stayed there for the entire allotted time, which was from 3:00-8:30 PM, making our visit about five and a half hours long. Before we left, he said a blessing to me- the same one he said every night before bed. You'll read it soon. We then exchanged our love and parted ways. Since we didn't leave the room once, Keith and I were feeling our call of duty and we rushed to the bathroom together. After gathering our things and thoughts, we went to grab some steaks on our way home. We talked a bit about what happened but I was still processing a lot and have never really done that verbally. There we sat eating our steak in silence.

*Dad's Letter*
*February 22, 2009*
*Dear Friend, Fay Key,*

    *You always seem so concerned about how I am doing so I will say right away that I am doing quite well. I've gained a circle of guys as friends that all pray for each other and keep each other encouraged. That helps a lot when we have to endure some of the difficult things of being in prison. I'll tell you more about some of the guys later.*

    *I'm glad to hear you are making it through this winter. One of the men that writes me from my church said that Western Michigan has gotten 108 inches of snow this winter so far. Good thing you had some thawing weather in there, otherwise most things would be covered. I imagine you are looking forward to spring. It has probably been a winter to stay inside but that gets old after a while.*

*My family has been able to make it over for visits once in a while. There has been so much snow I worry about them making the trip back and forth. However, when they can make it over for a visit, it is so good to see them. My mom and dad are in Florida for the winter so I have not seen them for a while but my brothers and sister have come over regularly.*

*I get updated on Bre and Christopher and the rest of the family from them. Bre is continuing at Calvin College. She went out east to the state of Maine and the Boston area for three weeks in January to study American Literature. It was a three week course through Calvin which she really enjoyed. The class was about 20-30 other students that all traveled together. Bre has always thrived on groups of kids her age so she had a great time. She may have even learned a thing or two while she was always having so much fun. I'm so glad we didn't really have TV when the kids were growing up because then we read so many books to them. Needless to say both of the kids were/are big readers. I thank God for that and the fact that both of them would read good material.*

*Chris is doing very well in his junior year in high school. He got all A's on his report card for the last semester even while working his job and being very active in school activities. He keeps his priorities just where they should be and makes sure he gets his homework done first before anything else. Of course his friends are still high on his list so he has a lot of fun with them too.*

*I sure miss being able to stop in to see you once in a while too. It always made my day so I could never figure out why more officers didn't do more of that. I've told some of my friends here about you as one of the blessings God has given me in this world. Thanks for staying in touch.*

*My brother Keith had a book called "The Shack"*

*mailed to me. If you get a chance to pick up a copy of "The Shack" somewhere I'm sure you would enjoy reading it very much. The story is about a man who lost his daughter and then later has an experience of spending a weekend with God at the shack where his young daughter was killed. It's a wonderful story about how God interacts with us and how his forgiveness can affect us. I've shared the book with several of my hurting friends here.*

*One of my friends here told me a while back that he is glad I am here. He feels really bad for what he did. He is past the point of wanting to take his own life now but he still goes through some tough times. I ran into him two days ago just by chance as he was coming back from a court appointment. He was quite down about what happened there but we got to talk to each other for a few minutes. Yesterday he said he was so glad that God made it so we could talk those few minutes because he really needed that encouragement from a Christian brother right at that point. We both commented that God still has a plan for the both of us wherever we are.*

*A week ago right after church another guy named came up to me and asked me to pray for him. He started to break down emotionally as he stood there because he said he is so scared and feels so bad for what he did that he has been considering suicide. Of course I could only talk to him a few minutes but I assured him that I would pray for him and ask my family and friends to do the same. He is doing a little better this week as I touched base with him but please include him in your prayers.*

*[A guy] from the U.P. asked me to pray for his wife and young son. He heard I was a Christian so asked for prayers on their behalf.*

*[He] is a guy a few years older than me and he has been a real blessing to me. I go to him for encouragement*

*so I thank God for him.*

*We had another wonderful church service this morning. There were just over 100 guys that came out for the service. I don't get to know many of them but it is good to see so many there and make some connections with them during the week when I get a chance. It's nice to be accountable for your actions during the week and to meet some of the guys I see in church. I hope you know that I pray for you everyday also. I cannot stop by and visit like I used to but I can pray for you and ask that God continue to bless you like He has for so many years already. God has blessed each of us so that we can be a bless to others so I hope He gives you many more years to be blessed and to be a blessing.*

*I trust your family is doing well. It sounds like they are around when you need them. My sister Beth's daughter was supposed to have a baby this weekend so their/our family is growing. That is her first grand child so it is a fun time for them.*

*God bless you,*
*Your Brother in Christ,*
*Ken*

*Dad's Letter*
*September 26, 2008*
*Dear Keith,*

*I got two of your letters yesterday. The one dated September 9 and September 22. Thanks for Toph's schedule. That helps me feel a little bit connected but most importantly I know what to pray for specifically. I also wrote his schedule on the [School] calendar I got from [a friend] too.*

*Wow the saltwater fish thing has me amazed! I could believe it would cost so much to fill it up. What on earth could cost so much? How many gallons was that? 500?*

*You wrote in your September 9 letter that the week before was a hard week for you with the kids starting school and the fact that everything was settling in so you were missing me. I miss you like crazy too and especially the kids. I'm starting to get a little use to it but I think it's more because I just don't think about it. Going to church for the first time in eight months was really hard this last week. We sang a couple of songs that I remember singing at [church] and I just couldn't sing without getting choked up. That will take some time to get use to that again but it will happen.*

*My roommate is a young hispanic that is a pretty good kid for a roommate. He has his TV down from his top bunk so I can see it too but the changes the channel at least every two minutes. We've never seen a whole show and most times we've never watched a show from one commercial break to the next. At least I have something to watch until I can get a TV. Hopefully I won't go crazy by then.*

*I don't know if [sister] let you know about what has to be done for visits so I'll tell you too and write [brother] also. I had to make up a list of immediate family that qualify and then up to ten friends... But before anyone can visit they have to fill out a form. It can be done online or it has to be sent in. If it's mailed in, it would be best to put a self addressed envelope in so they will let you know if it's approved or not. Otherwise I could see getting all the way out here and someone isn't approved.*

*Thanks for the e-journal from [church]. Yeah I'm struggling with God about some things too. Someday I hope to share that with you.*

*I'm getting to know a few more of the Christian guys in my building. That has been great to have someone that I feel I have something in common with. Not that I get to talk to them all that much but It's something and they are helping me get set up with everything here. I'm still keeping a low profile with all of them but I'm still not afraid of anything coming back on me.*

*I got a letter from Mom and Dad, and three from the Dowlers with a whole a whole bunch of catholic info in it. They are so great. It's good to be getting mail again. I still can't use the phone for some reason but hopefully soon. I don't know what the hold up is but everything takes a while here it seems.*

*I love you brother.*
*Love Ken*

*Dad's Letter*
*July 2, 2012*
*Dear Toph,*
*This card comes with all the birthday well wishing that is possible. I imagine you living it up in Chicago all the time so I cannot imagine you being any better of or having more fun that what you are now. You are turning twenty-one so now you can have your first beer! Yea right. I know better than that. All I care about is that you are smart about about that; and I know you are. That makes me recall a memory from when you were about eleven or twelve. It was toward the end of Hope's exams and there was a Hope student house with a big afternoon party at it. I had worked that day and stopped in to talk to some kids I know and make sure they kept a lid on it so it didn't get out of hand. They were having a great time and were good kids so I said I might stop in after work. They said they would watch for me. I went home first, picked you up to work out at the gym and we stopped in at that outdoor party for a few minutes. After we left you were disgusted that, "Those kids were*

*drinking bee-ah!" I just smiled and thought, "You wait." You had almost always hung out with kids older than you were and since that probably wouldn't be changing at all your friends would be able to drink much sooner than you could legally. That's why I was glad you were so smart about stuff like that and I wanted to do what I could to help you stay that way.*

*Speaking of smarts- I hope you like this card. A friend of mine makes cards so I told him a few things about you and asked him to see what he could come up with. The bunch of guys he hangs out with always kid me about doubling the total of the IQ at the table when I come to it. They are kidding (you already know that because this is me we're talking about) but we often tell stories of the stupid things guys here say. Here are a few of the highlights. One guy asked me, "Where is West America?" He figured there is North America and a South America, so there must be a West America. There is another story about someone else who was geographically challenged. He was watching that Atlanta Falcons football game and asked, "Atlanta Georgia- is that in Florida?" Oh, there was the guy from Muskegon who didn't know that Lake Michigan was so big that it went "all the way down to Holland." You can see why this place makes me feel smart sometimes. You know what they say, "In a kingdom of blind men, a one eyed man is king."*

*I told my buddies, that group of them, about you working at the Chicago Planetarium so he picked up on the idea of "Searching to find intelligent life." I hope you are really enjoying your job there. I imagine that you are learning a lot working there. I'm picking up whatever planetary information I can so I can know a little something but I think you probably by now learned and forgotten more than I could ever get my hands on. Please just don't become so smart and as stupid all the same time like Steven Hawkings. As incredibly smart he is he still says that all the cosmos he has never seen any proof of there being a God. I can't imagine not seeing proof.*

*Speaking of Steven Hawkings, did you see him on "The Big Bang Theory?" That was so funny! I love that show. Sheldon always reminds me of Grandpa and I laugh at so much at the show. I seldom miss it on Thursday nights.*

*I was wondering the other day if you would need to change your state of residency from Michigan to Illinois. There was a time that I thought Bre would do something like that before you would but on the other hand you surprised and amazed me about so many things so many times that I guess I never gave enough credit to how strong your sense of curiosity and drive to gain knowledge is. Grandma sent me the article from the Zeeland Paper about you being on the dean's list at Columbia College which says a lot about what curiosity can do for someone. You being a science journalist will be one person who is curious sharing with other people who want to live curiously.*

*A few friends came for a visit a few weeks ago. They come every few months so we catch up on what is going on with everyone and have some good laughs. It was great fun to tell them that you were living in an apartment with three girls all summer. He laughed and said he couldn't wait to tell [his son] because he would be so jealous. You may already know but [his son] is at Calvin and of course [your other friend] is at Hope. I forget what their summer jobs were but I don't imagine their jobs were as cool as working at the Planetarium.*

*About six months ago there was a guy here who had graduated from Harold Washington about ten years ago with, I guess a music degree, because he was an opera singer. He was a huge black guy, 6'3" about 350 lbs, but not really fat. He got transferred before I knew you were going to transfer to HW. I wish he was still here because he would have been thrilled to hear about you going to his Alma Mater. He loved talking about downtown Chicago and all the cool stuff to do. Now that I pay attention to it I realize how many shots of Chicago they show on TV. And you are right in the middle of it.*

*Besides the Calvin class I'm taking and the Celebration Fellowship Church a few of us started with a few weeks ago, I'm also meeting with twelve other guys in a Social Entrepreneurial start up group. It's mostly older guys but some are young and very mature guys who want to show some of the idiots here that they don't have to stay that way. That has been an interesting bunch. We had Kirk Cousins come here last June.*

*Well Toph, I think of you often and pray for you several times a day. I hope you enjoy life, work hard because you like it, and love your family, friends, and yourself.*

*Love Dad*


Like I said, life in prison seems to be treating him well. It could be because that is all he will tell me and in general he doesn't like to be a downer. Too many times, I have heard him say, "I don't like to complain." Even when there is silt in his tap water; even when his meals make a public schools hot lunch look like five star surf and turf. He frequently reassures everyone he is safe and finds ways to kill time by reading books, writing, watching TV and taking classes. I've tried to get him to tell me about some of the things that are bothering him to see if it is something fixable. If you have ever seen *Orange is the New Black* on

Netflix, you'll get an appropriate view of the things he describes: overcrowding, real meals turned to precooked bags, unmotivated unionized CO's mistreating people, and lack of facility upkeep. I would like to fix these, but have no idea how. There's even a Lauren Lapkus-like character CO: scrawny with kind eyes- the kind of person that looks like they should be leading a daycare for children, not grown-ass criminals. I've mentioned that show to him and described all the terms about prison culture they mention in the show. He was surprised at how much I knew and how I was throwing around terms like Commissary and CO. Commissary is a prison multi-mart at which you can buy anything from a radio to Top Ramen, the popular prison currency, not to be confused with the plebeian regular Raman or Cup of Noodles.

Communication with my father comes and goes. I ended up visiting him a few more times over the years with various other people: friends and a pastor from the DeKleine family church. We've talked a lot about life and forgiveness and moving on; about how eventually you have to stop talking about it and start doing it. My last visit with him was before I went on my big trip in September 2015. I made sure to see him one last time because I had no idea when it will happen again but it did and my latest visit was Christmas time of 2017.

Ken is in his third prison right now. The government likes to keep people moving so they don't get too comfortable but sometimes they let the prisoners with good behavior stick around if they are close to their family. There is still always a chance he could be shipped off. When I saw him before I left, it was a surprise so he didn't know why he was being called to the front desk. The guards aren't allowed tell the prisoners where they are going so the inmates can't plan anything and he told me that while he was walking with the guards, he wondered if he was going to get moved to another prison again. Even when they relocate him, they don't tell him anything about what is happening. When he was transported from the east side of the state to the west side a few years ago, the one thing he knew was that he was going west- only because of the setting sun. Since this was towards home, he kept hoping they would continue all the way to the other side and they did.

In the past year, he's told me about prison emails. Since I travel a lot, we've only been using the prison email system JPay. This is much more convenient than writing letters and buying stamps, although admittedly the emails I receive are less detailed, thought out, and more typo ridden than the letters. He has a time limit on the computers so he is in more of a rush but I still get to let him know about where I am and send pictures once a month or so. At first I didn't think this was enough, but figured I've got all the time in the world and he'll be there.

Not many people ask him what his life is like in prison. Maybe it's because they don't want to hear it, maybe it's because they don't know how to ask it, maybe it's because they think he doesn't want to talk about it. He does, at least that's what he tells me. His first and only job so far is working in the kitchen with a starting wage of 27¢ an hour but has gotten a two-cent raise since then and maybe more but money isn't incredibly useful in prison unless you want to by candy bars with a few days pay and if you get too flashy, people are going to steal your shit, which has already happened to him. He works late night shift cooking for the guards so he gets to eat all the food he wants, which is becoming more obvious, and gets to sleep during the day. Apparently the guards love his food, especially his home made french dressing and even joke around saying the only reason they would catch him if he escaped was to bring back his amazing french dressing.

Regardless of what the movies make you think, it is safe in prison. They are like any city in the sense it all depends on where you go; there are places to avoid, but apparently it's really easy to avoid them. Roommates have come and gone, some good, some bad. Some steal his stuff or make prison hooch, which is not okay to joke about in the visiting room by the way; learned that one the hard way. I cracked a joke about hooch in the visiting room and my dad immediately tensed up, looked around and told me not to mention it. *Whoops.*

He has made friends and there are many good people in prison, believe it or not. It's gotten to the point where he started introducing me to whatever friends are in the visiting room. One of his friends is even painting a portrait of my sister and her husband in exchange for a blanket crocheted by my dad. Apparently the black market in prison also has art (even though they aren't allowed to barter and trade.) Everyone in there has a story and I can't help but think about it all when I sit amongst them. Sometimes it's hard to focus on our conversation. This past visit, around Christmas it was us, two modest Dutch Boys, sitting in between a prison tranny and a visibly actual White Supremacist, with SS tattoos and all. Maybe they wouldn't be there if someone listened to them, believed in them, if they were born to a different family or went to a different school, or maybe they just were in the wrong place at the wrong time and got screwed by a severely flawed system. Either way, they are where they are and dwelling on it is not going to help anyone.

Prison also has various classes and seminars. He mentions taking a seminary class through a local college and even took a creative writing course, which I love asking him about. It's fun to hear him struggle with fabricating characters and stories because he's never been one for that kind of thing. I mean, he got me into Lord of the Rings and Star Wars, but was never much of an artist or creator himself so I encourage him to flex his creativity. Currently he has graduated to the point of teaching a class to prisoners through Calvin College, a local Christian school in west Michigan.

Otherwise I hear a lot about the shows he likes and keeps up to date with- one of his "guilty pleasure" shows being *The Walking Dead*. We never had real television growing up so he jokes about how this is the first time in his life he's had easy access to cable. Television shows also give us something light to talk about. I try and make sure he is exercising, considering he just passed the same age at which his father died of a heart attack. Also, the extra cheeseburgers he gets to eat weren't exactly helping his waste line. I hope he gets to read this. Between encouraging him with his art, reminding him to go for a walk occasionally, and checking in on him and his friends, sometimes it feels like I'm the parent now.

When the first visit came around, I decided full disclosure on everything. Now that his effect on my life is completely up to me, as is everything really, it was the time for the best of policies: honesty. I told him about receiving my Medical Marijuana Card in Michigan. He was a little skeptical at first, the next time I saw him, he said he spoke with a friend whose son was doing the same thing and actually convinced her it was okay to do… because I was doing it. *Who are you?* Although I don't feel the need to partake anymore. He has become blindly supportive of everything I do without regard to what it is. He's now one of the very few "adults" in my life where justification for the decisions I make isn't necessary, considering I biked across the country and visiting Myanmar for two months. Even if it means a visitation won't be possible for a long time, he is nothing but encouraging and sticks up for me when people ask what the hell I'm doing and why. Frequently I'll email him about what I'm doing across the world and apparently "people are living through me on my latest adventures," and he says he loves telling people these things, despite the many questions of why. It's curious how his body being locked up has been able to free his mind so much.

On July 16th, 2016 I said the most difficult things I've ever said in my life to my father: "You did the right thing." This is a conclusion I have been orbiting for years and it is tough to admit, but if I didn't say it I would by lying. Lying by omission is still lying. It wasn't easy to say murdering my mother was the right choice. It wasn't easy to admit to myself that my mother, my sister's mother, my grandparents daughter et cetera needed to be put down for my life to begin. I love my grandparents and that side of the family so much, but I have to be honest about this. I have to. I'm not proud to say it. It sure as shit doesn't make me happy and doesn't fill any void. It doesn't make me sad either. It just is.

It may be a long time until I see my dad again but I know we'll keep in touch and I'm sure he'll be there when I get back. It's not like he's going anywhere.

*7/21/2016*
*Dear Toph,*
*Other than being a little sleep deprived I have been on Cloud 9 all week. First and foremost from knowing that you are doing so well in CA and enjoying life so much. The second reason is from our phone talk and your letter which gave me an incredible boost of validation of what I thought*

*was going on 10 years ago and what I hoped you would come to understand. I cannot describe the pain I felt while reading an email from mom in which she says how you and Bre will hate me and piss on my grave if I didn't stop having suspicions of John Does and her (paraphrased). Being called a coward was hard to take. Now you gave me the validation I waited for, enduring her accusations and the trial that painted me as - _____ - no words can describe- other than the worst person around and a monster, it was hard to take. At sentencing, the judge said my case was the worst one he ever presided over. I don't blame him since the prosecutor painted a horrendous image of me which didn't get any defense against or objections. So hearing and reading about you doing so well, loving life, living an adventure others could only dream of, makes me swell with joy for you and pride in you. You and I have been through the fire- and been refined.*

*A lighter subject- the reason for my sleep deprivation is that it is the final week for the Calvin guys' writing class. The prof has come every morning this week at 7:30 AM so when I work until 23:30 or 2:00 AM, it's kind of difficult getting up for class. I'm the only person as the Teacher's Assistant that can print stuff off, so for this writing class, the guys need papers printed every morning. Thankfully I have no problem napping in the afternoon. Yesterday, after putting my earplugs in and my eye cover on, I slept from 12:15 to 3:45. They said a storm came through but I was clueless about it.*

*I got your letter. Your right about actually writing letters, hand written, and receiving hand written letters which have a certain quality to them that no other form of rhetoric has. Another good thing is that you can stop writing whenever and pick it up whenever and wherever you want. This will take me a few days so I'll get it out*

Monday.

*Saturday Afternoon:* I'm sitting in Study Hall, the classroom for Calvin, and marveling at the absurdity of the MDOC [Michigan Department of Corrections]. Last summer, the MDOC promised they would have A/C for the Calvin profs and the classroom. Last year! This summer came and still nothing so they cobbled one small A/C for this big room. That did nothing. Then they got two more units and they can't keep up in this heat either. Guys sit huddled around the blowers to keep cool. One year and they still don't have a real A/C system.

Speaking of this incredible heat wave, I'm trying to think of a good metaphor for describing what it has been like for me since our talk on the phone and getting your letter. I feel like my spirit has been getting bathed in cool spring waters by that you said and wrote. I've shared a few things you said with a few guys that respect me, or I should say, guys that respected me even before. I don't want to share it unless they've already respected me because I don't want to get in my mind that I've earned their respect by what I shared with them. So all week I've been basking in the realization that I've matured so much in that last few years. No not really, but that you have matured so much in the last year. Matured enough to deal with and delve into a risky emotional topic. And to keep digging. I'll take the chance of you finding out some unflattering things about me. But I think you have rattled the bones of all my skeletons.

I've read and reread your letter several times now. You are correct about me feeling uncomfortable about brining up the subject about what lead up to and me actually taking the drastic actions I did but that is only because I did not want to broach the subject before you were ready. Pushing you in a way or lead you where you *didn't want to go would not have been good for you I felt. To me it would be better to let you discover what you wanted, when you wanted. Then it would be your own achievement as you climb up the mountain, at your own pace, on the route of your choice, and with whom you choose.*

*So as you say, I "Did the right thing." I've often thought in the last eight years "I would serve ten life sentences to stop what Bre and Topher were and would have to endure for who knows how long. And after destroying Doe's family she would move on to destroy another." So by the end of January 2007 I was quite sure I'd have to take some drastic action. I continued to pray that Lori would have a change of heart, or that something else would happen, but it never did. For a year I struggled with what mom "committing suicide" would do to you and Bre and everyone else. I also struggled with what it would do to my conscience and whether I wanted to yoke myself with that burden- by myself, without ever being able to tell anyone. I know I made decisions before about, not if someone was going to die, but how many, however this was different. It was close to my two kids I love, involve someone I loved in the past, and would have huge ripple effects. No matter what happened I had to have faith and trust in you and Bre that you would eventually mature to the point of getting it.*

*(A few hours later- I had to proof read someone's paper.)*

*All that to say, "I'm comfortable with anything you want to talk about, ask about, and at some point I may spring something on you that you were unaware of."*

*[...]*

*Sorry, I jump around so much, or my mind does, as I sit here pondering your letter again. (By the way, it was* nice hearing what you said on the phone, more like awesome, and then reading what you wrote in your letter.) I was reminded about something [Friend] said during late 2006 or 2007 by what you said about moms manipulation. I had told her and [her husband] about how embarrassed I was by how much Lori and had been able to fool me for so many years. She said it was probably good that I had gone to Iraq for a year to get out from under Lori's insidious maneuverings of you and Bre, as well as me and so many other people. She said she could see how after being gone for a year I had a clearer view of how Lori would control people. When I started pointing it out to other people, even [mom's coworker] said she saw Lori as a "master manipulator." But by then, Lori had everyone at church walking on eggshells, afraid of what she would do if they went against her and fired her. [Another coworker] referred to "walking on eggshells" around Lori from way back when they worked together as a team job sharing. So my point is that it took me being gone fore a year to figure out something wasn't right which means I can completely understand why it took you a while to figure it out since you were sixteen at the time and that is all you ever knew in your life. That reminds me of what Jan said at the end of January 2007 when I told her all I wanted was for you and Bre to have a normal life- Jan said, "Ken, your kids have never had a normal life."

    You wrote about how I was silenced and ignored by too many people. That is some very incredible insight. What are some of you recollections of that? More importantly, when were you silenced and ignored about it? And are you silenced and ignored about it now? There is a find line between ignoring and unrelatability.

    [...]

    Well Toph, if the silent language of the heart could be

*heard, the words "I love you" would swell up from deep within me, burst forth from my spirit, sweep across the plains we've traversed, reverberate off the mountains we've trodden, cross the canyons we've descended into, and by means only known to the ether world, make it to the ears of your heart. My prayer is that your hearts ear will hear the echo of "I love you" until the last vital drop visits my heart and that you know I am your greatest well-wisher as well as encourager of all your undertakings. Hear my heart oh ye mighty master of the palette and brush! May you feel my spirit standing next to you on the right, for it is with my left hand that I carry my shield. As a warrior said 2,400 years ago:*

> *This is my shield,*
> *I bear it before me into battle,*
> *But it is not mine alone.*
> *It protects my brother on my left*
> *And it protects my city.*
> *I will not let my brother fall from*
> *It's shadow or my city from it's protection.*
> *If need be I will die with my shield before me, facing the enemy.*

*God bless,*
*Dad*


Upon the visit during Christmas of 2017, I had one more pressing question after writing this book and doing all this research.

Why did you choose to be with and marry her?

His answer was because she was the only one who would go camping with him. She was the only one that would dare to go on crazy adventures and was up for anything at all times. Because she was the only one for him. "I still cannot imagine meeting anybody like your mom ever again."

*Back to the surreal summer of 1988. We went to a few marriage counseling sessions that summer. Ironically it was right where John Doe's office was. I remember, after the therapist met with mom alone first, he met alone with me. He advised me point blank just to get a divorce. I'm still glad I didn't. Don't ever think that I may regret not cutting my losses right away back then. Just as pure complete sorrow is as possible as pure and complete joy, the opposite of that is possible - which is to be completely sure that a decision made in the past, that resulted in two wonderful benefits, is not a regretted choice.*

I chose to forgive and love my mother and father for the terrible things they have individually caused in my life. Not only do I forgive them but I am grateful for what they blessed me with: life. For life is what finds a way to overcome Death and All Her Friends. However I cannot take the fully hippy dippy stance that love is all I need nor is it the only thing I can give. Hatred for John Doe and his intentional misguidance is something I have to now live with. Pray I don't see him on the Holland sidewalk again lest I receive the same fate as my father.

"If only it were all so simple! If only there were evil people somewhere insidiously committing evil deeds, and it were necessary only to separate them from the rest of us and destroy them. But the line dividing good and evil cuts through the heart of every human being. And who is willing to destroy a piece of his own heart?" - Aleksandr Solzhenitsyn

That leaves me with the question, "How do I deal with this? How do I deal with this evil piece of my own heart?" I can't track down John and burn his house to the ground hoping he remains inside. I know that if I remain diligent, I can take that energy and redirect it. Redirect it towards something beneficial both for myself as an individual and to others. I can take that fury to the keyboard in the hope that this story will serve as a lesson to the people of this world that are struggling with their inner balance of good and evil and for them I pray.

This has taken me ten years almost to the exact date to put these pieces back together and into words, having been written on January 7, 2018. It has taken me ten years to realize that this fury is not something I can cure through changing friends, changing location, changing jobs, changing the chemicals in my very brain. It has taken me ten years to realize this fury, this evil that we all struggle with is a struggle that cannot be done alone. I need something Greater than myself in which to believe. I need an idea of perfection, the Idol of Christ, to strive for in order to give me Hope and meaning. Without a destination, where am I to direct my journey?

My dad asked me during Christmas of 2017, "In your manuscript you said mom deserved what she received, does that mean I deserve to be where I am?" Deserve is such a judgmental word to use because who am I to say anyone deserves anything? Then I thought of something my Aunt Jan wrote- who deserves this credit- it's not that we do or don't deserve anything, rather we are CHOSEN. My family and I have been CHOSEN to bear this burden so that we may overcome it together through Grace and share it with others. It has taken me twenty-six years, three months, and nine days to realize this life will work out just fine.

*Dad's Letter*

*January 26, 2008*
*Dear Bre and Toph,*
*Last week I found these Blessing in the book I was reading- Our Father Abraham. I copied them and I have them with me all the time. Whenever you get these or are ready to receive them, know that I mean them for you. If you are not ready to accept these from me for a long time, weeks, month, or years, please know that I have felt this way all the time.*

*Bre: "May God make you like Sarah, Rebekah, Rachel, and Leah*
> *May the Lord bless you and keep you.*
> *May the Lord make His face to shine upon you, and be gracious to you.*
> *May the Lord lift up his countenance upon you, and give you peace (shalom)."*

*Toph: "May god make you like Ephraim and Manasseh.*
> *May the Lord bless you and keep you.*
> *May the Lord make His face shine upon you, and be gracious to you.*
> *May the Lord lift up his countenance upon you, and give you peace (shalom)."*

*I love you both*
*Dad*

Made in the USA
Lexington, KY
05 February 2018